"The fire in your belly for best in class, ROI driven digital marketing is evident on every page. While we are not a high value B to C item, *The CEO's Digital Marketing Playbook* has given me executable and strategic insights to achieve more profit from our digital and social marketing. I am taking lessons learned from the book into action items at NuGo immediately."

—**David Levine**, CEO NuGo Nutrition

"*The CEO's Digital Marketing Playbook* is a practical and enjoyable guide that aims to help executives answer the question, 'How do I maximize the ROI from our marketing budget?'

"The Playbook also provides a window into current trends and terminology in digital marketing, an area that can be intimidating or inaccessible to execs of boring old-economy businesses; such as myself. Donohoe walks the walk and talks the talk in this well-written and concise marketing resource for business leaders."

—**Charlie Walsh**, EVP of Sales and Marketing, Stephenson Equipment

"Donohoe provides a battle tested guide for the C-Suite Executive on how to not be distracted by gimmicky marketing tactics. In doing so, he empowers each to call bullshit on misdirected, off-point ideas that can drain cash from our businesses."

—**James D. Ewing, Jr.**, CEO | President, COE DISTRIBUTING

The CEO's DIGITAL
MARKETING PLAYBOOK:

The Definitive Crash Course and Battle Plan for
B2B and High Value B2C Customer Generation

by Thomas J. Donohoe

© Copyright 2019 Thomas J. Donohoe

ISBN 978-1-63393-950-9

Published by

 köehlerbooks™

210 60th Street
Virginia Beach, VA 23451
800−435−4811
www.koehlerbooks.com

THE CEO'S DIGITAL MARKETING PLAYBOOK

The Definitive Crash Course and Battle Plan for B2B and High Value B2C Customer Generation

THOMAS J. DONOHOE

VIRGINIA BEACH
CAPE CHARLES

This book is dedicated to Ann Donohoe.

You showed generations of our family the spirit to endure,
the grace to provide, and the wisdom of a steady hand.

THE MARKETER'S RAISON D'ETRE

Q: WHAT IS THE GOAL OF MARKETING?

A: To sell more products and services, ideally, where (a) there is a return on marketing investment and where (b) your company makes a net profit.

That's it.

It is the only reason executives draw this arrow from management quivers and deploy departments and resources that are dedicated to the science and art of marketing.

The goals are simple. More leads and qualified sales opportunities. and a higher profit and a Return on Marketing Investment. At the end of each month, quarter, and year . . . those are the goals and they must not be abandoned in lieu of more casual and less essential causes.

Your mission *isn't* the following: Awards for the prettiest website or most viral commercial, although those are nice plaques to rest on the reception desk and make a sweet email signature. It's not clicks and not impressions, though these days that is often the extent of marketing "performance" reports. The goal isn't the most transcendent customer journey and it sure the heck isn't getting the most likes on Facebook or retweets. Most importantly, it is certainly not the hundreds of other things marketers and agencies talk about when not talking about increased sales and ROI.

If your marketing team is only talking about impressions, clicks, and "likes" on Facebook, then you are setting money on fire. This playbook's job is, directly and simply without the nonsensical cheerleading and hype of most business books, to tell you what to do to change that.

As a call to arms and convenient definition, what we are going to preach and show its rightful place in your marketing world, is **Customer Generation Marketing.**

To double down on this, I would contend that any *other* kind of marketing is a waste of time and money.

Marketing is about turning people into customers—new customers or, even better, repeat ones. That means everything in marketing needs to be a direct, accountable, ROI+ strategy. If it's not achieving that goal, and aiming hard and straight for ROI, then you must question its value.

It really is that simple: a huge percentage of a CEO or CMO's marketing mindshare, let alone the stuff that people in marketing departments are paid to do on a daily basis, is focused on things *other* than activities *directly* tied to customer generation.

This book is a battle plan to ensure that you understand the essential pieces of 21st Century Marketing that are the throbbing heart of customer generation, and how to ensure each piece is present and accounted for in your business.

Most importantly, this is a conversation for the forgotten majority—the men and women who run companies in the B2B or High Value B2C verticals (High Value means goods and services that are expensive and take longer than five minutes to sell).

This is an attempt to talk about 1) marketing missing the point of ROI, and 2) the thousands of B2B and High Value B2C companies that aren't the target of most larger marketing books and agencies and global focus. Why? Because your business—one with a sales cycle greater than a five-minute click to purchase on Amazon—are harder to do well in from a marketing standpoint. The goals and customer path are harder to craft as they span weeks, months and sometimes years. Adding to the challenge is the fact that your B2B or High Value B2C company likely spends much less than mass market B2C companies like Coke and McDonald's who deploy huge, untargeted brand marketing budgets like a caffeinated Oprah giving away stuff on a Christmas special. When is the last time a brand marketer talked about ROI at a campaign level compared to how often you worry about how many new customers every penny is driving?

So, we want to talk to you about how to fix what's *not* happening in your marketing and sales funnel and do it in the next hundred or so pages. Because you've been ignored long enough.

I don't have Ten Commandments in my marketing world.

I have one: **X Dollars = Y Results.**

That's it.

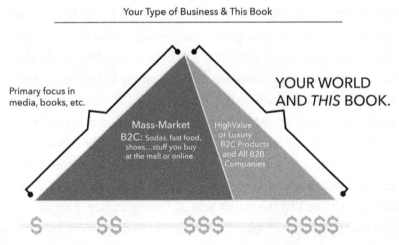

Your Type of Business & This Book

Primary focus in media, books, etc.

YOUR WORLD AND *THIS* BOOK.

Mass-Market B2C: Sodas, fast food, shoes...stuff you buy at the mall or online.

HighValue or Luxury B2C Products and All B2B Companies

$ $$ $$$ $$$$

The sliding scale of cheaper to more expensive products and services

WHY I'M HERE

A QUICK STORY TO TELL YOU why I wrote this and why I'm here.

In the early 2000s (like, the *early* 2000s) I got my first job in digital advertising on Wall Street. Technically, it was on Old Slip Street a few blocks away, but my mom doesn't know that one, so there you go.

And the deal was as simple as it was both irresistible and suffering. They'd pay me, a kid with a decent undergrad degree and some marketing work but zero point zero knowledge of this new thing called digital advertising, $31,500 a year. In Manhattan. And for this handsome sum, which unquestionably meant that I spent my tenure with that company sleeping in a hostel on East 7th Street, they would teach me everything they knew about effective tactics in customer generation and digital advertising just as this industry was being born. If I shut my mouth, worked twelve- to fifteen-hour days, they'd teach me the black magic of using ads online to drive customers to what became (and still is) the leader in B2C foreign currency trading. My new job would be to deploy dollars online to drive more customers at a good cost per acquisition to *their* company vs. their competition.

I was sold as fast as a bro orders a Jager-bomb. During homecoming.

And from day one, my new cohort of fresh-faced and blank-slate digital media buyers and I worked our young asses off and twice a week would sit in front of the Chief Marketing Officer himself and be taught the Ninja skills of digital advertising: buying and negotiating on a cost per click or cost per milli basis; what needed to happen after a person gets to the website to turn them into a new client; backing out the most important KPIs—the cost to acquire a new client—using the money we spent on a specific campaign as the numerator and the number of new clients won as the denominator; making sure that the *right* people were being targeted and that we were using the most effective tools in search engine and banner advertising for our company (social networks weren't invented yet!).

And when you read this, all this took place about twenty years ago. I'm not old by general professional standards, but I'm a grandfather in the digital advertising space. 100 percent.

And what blows my mind—and the reason I'm here—is that now, *twenty years later*, two things are true:

1. The stuff I learned back then still works and is the foundation for nearly everything else that can most effectively drive new customers through your B2B or High Value B2C company's sales funnel.
2. Very few companies are doing it well, likely including yours.

To me, that's insane.

The internet is real. Digital advertising is the best, most cost-effective vehicle to win new business in B2B and High Value B2C. And you need to be doing the baseline things I was shown before *Friends* was a TV show and *Cheers* and *M*A*S*H* were still on prime time.

I run a multimillion-dollar digital advertising agency that's been on the INC 500 list, and both the agency and I have won a bunch of other awards that look very fancy in the lobby of our headquarters. What I want to share with you is that aside from my family, I care more about smart digital marketing than anything else in the world, and I've done nothing else professionally aside from dedicating my life to knowing more than any other CEO running a digital marketing agency. That's a hard promise.

And I want to teach you everything I've learned in building a career and company in digital and direct marketing. I want to tell you in these 240 or so pages about both the essential four things (The Core Four) for every company to do tomorrow morning and, if they're already at that level, do the group of more advanced things (The Advanced Eight) that will allow them to beat their competition.

This Playbook is divided into five components: an introduction to the commanding philosophy of good digital marketing, and four chapters laying out everything critical you need to know to do two things. One, to ensure that good 21st Century Marketing is being done under your watch *vis a vis* arming you with enough education to be able to manage in-house experts or an agency. Two, if you run a smaller company or are one of the marketers in the trenches doing the work, this will give you a real step-by-step playbook for exactly what to do to deploy both the essential tactics as well as some more advanced campaigns that are the lower hanging fruit of profitable digital and direct marketing.

TABLE OF CONTENTS

THE KINGDOM AND THE POWER OF DIGITAL DIRECT RESPONSE

WE MUST NOT, AS EXECUTIVES and professionals dedicated to profitable business outcomes, miss the mark and real opportunities in what the 21st Century has afforded us the ability to achieve in customer generation. Most marketing agencies employ tactics and strategies that are for clients and companies with old, bad habits:

1. They spend millions of dollars on brand advertising (and therefore make their agencies, who charge clients based on a percentage of media spend, rather rich)
2. They don't focus on direct response or ROI and don't hold their marketers accountable for profitability—and are therefore the dream accounts.

If you're reading this, ***that's likely not your business.***

WHO THIS BOOK IS FOR

This book is for the C-Level professional, marketing or otherwise, who needs to confirm that her or his marketing departments are doing the right, best practice things that in 2020 and beyond are highly correlated with a positive Marketing ROI. This is for a VP of Marketing who just changed jobs into an industry that demands more ROI accountability and direct response results than her previous job. This is for anyone who needs to know the bottom line, best practice, short and long-term, day-in-day-out marketing activities that represent the foundation for 21st Century direct and digital marketing that is the beating heart of customer generation.

This playbook is for leaders of companies in either the B2B world or High Value B2C industries where the net present value (NPV) of a new customer is a least a few hundred bucks. With all due respect to the complexity of lower price point B2C industries (think: things that cost a few bucks and are mass marketed to millions) where brand marketing still reigns supreme—as it doesn't make sense to unleash advanced digital advertising or direct marketing techniques and build your sales pipeline—the world of B2B and High Value B2C has changed absolutely and completely since 2001.

This is for CEOs and CMOs who hear more about impressions and clicks and "likes" on Facebook from their teams and agencies than Return on Advertising Spend or intelligent mid-funnel KPIs like Cost Per Qualified Lead.

This is a short and to-the-point battle plan for the CEO who has a dozen different teams and needs to know what to demand and how to ask for it. This is for VPs/C Level leaders looking to solve the DefCon 1 Problems vs. what can wait for later, what are the essential pieces to creating an efficient marketing and sales pipeline vs. the nice-to-have features which are fine for long-term strategy.

And this is for small business owners or sole proprietors, or the men and women in the marketing trenches for large companies, who really need a step-by-step playbook on what to do in 21st Century Marketing and exactly how to do it.

Most importantly, I want to teach you which marketing tactics make money and which are simply nice-to-have window dressing marketing activities. And to that end, there are plenty, make no mistake.

I want you to board a flight in JFK and arrive in LAX with the battlefield triage list of Must-Do tactics, the core strategy, and the right questions to ask to make sure your marketing teams are running in the right direction.

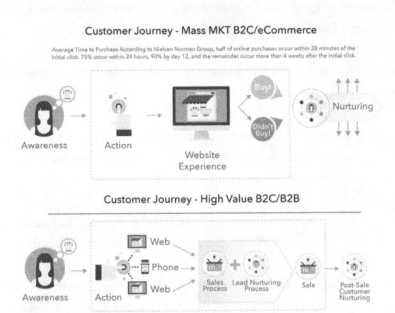

Customer Journey - Mass MKT B2C/eCommerce

Average Time to Purchase According to Nielsen Norman Group, half of online purchases occur within 28 minutes of the initial click. 75% occur within 24 hours, 90% by day 12, and the remainder occur more than 4 weeks after the initial click.

Customer Journey - High Value B2C/B2B

Unlike B2C eCommerce, the average sales cycle can be 2 weeks to 2 years

WHAT WE FOCUS ON

This playbook is not a State of The Union of digital and direct marketing, nor some abstract white paper or love letter to business strategies measured in quarters and years. This aims to discuss, dissect, and re-direct real rubber on the road tactics that your teams execute every day, spending your budget and taking your mindshare, and marketing line items that need to produce on a daily and weekly basis or else people lose their jobs.

I've done little else in my career other than customer generation focused marketing, most of it in digital channels, and plenty of it before I started an agency. I was the guy with the headphones on in the cubicle trenches who had one job: Spend marketing dollars to drive more customers and more revenue. And do it profitably. My teams—and I personally—have spent over $100 million on the client and agency side in the relentless pursuit to generate customers, and I've tested every channel with my fingers on the keyboard doing the work, and I need to tell you: it is *hard*.

I often wished, as a direct response, profit- and data-driven marketer, that I had a job on the other side of the rainbow. On the brand-building side of marketing,

- Where every opinion of every executive is a worthy strategy.
- Where the copywriting ideas and creative brainstorming sessions can trump data instead of data leading the conversation.
- Where numbers are discussed, oft times with words like "impressions" and "shares" and "likes" and "views," but rarely in scary terms like "Return on Advertising Spend" or "campaign ROI."
- Where the ghost of Don Draper proudly walks around with a glass of scotch at 11 am—past the hyper-colored "think pods," organic juice bar, and free shiatsu—nodding proudly as he sees his ethos of ROI unaccountability sink its teeth into every client's media budget and sees his face on every billboard, expensive TV commercial, and PR department.

And while all of this happens—at your company's agency or marketing department and in hundreds of other companies just like yours who need to make plans and profit every quarter—we as business professionals have lost sight of the goal of customer generation. We have failed to hold our internal marketing teams and our agencies accountable.

We—or maybe the pervasive marketing culture in general—have missed the mark.

Maybe we *think* we haven't, but we certainly waste 95 percent of our time talking about other things *not* related to ROI and customer generation when we talk about marketing. And we let our marketers and our agencies lead us down this path, billing hours and waxing poetic about long tail strategies and branding brands.

This is not saying brands do not have value. They do. Or that doing things that can help elevate your brand and build an audience for the long term aren't valuable. They are. But all too often, we invest too heavily in activities that are less about mathematically probable ROI and driving action and more about long-term creative strategies that all too often fail to drive net new activity. We focus 90 percent of the time on brand and 10 percent or less on deploying, optimizing, and nailing down, every day, the best practice direct response tactics that actually work in a direct cause and (revenue) effect relationship.

Why? Because deploying purely creative tasks is often easier than technology-based direct response customer generation. The platforms change, skills are harder to find than creative professionals, and *oh, my goodness* there is a quantifiable risk you might fail.

Bad creative? Maybe that's the product's fault or the sales team's fault or the supply chain's fault or someone/anyone else's fault

Bad direct response? That's all *you*, your marketing agency or your internal marketing team.

No wonder we hate doing it so much.

In the hard world where actions and results can be measured, who in the world wouldn't want to be Don Draper vs. the team whose job it is to put astronauts on the moon? If Don Draper fails, the creative strategy *never* gets the final blame.

But miss the moon and everyone knows which team's math was wrong.

In the world I live in, it's harder. Harder to find talent. Harder to keep up with ever-changing ad platforms and smart competition.

Harder to wake up every morning and know 100 percent that if your team doesn't drive X new actions at a Y cost per action, you're in for a hard conversation.

But in a budget battle, when things are tough and line items need to get prioritized, when we're talking about nice-to-have vs. need-to-have and stuff has to be cut, here is what's going to start happening in companies around the world as CEOs and CMOs get smarter:

- Pretty ad campaign brainstorming sessions and customer experience meetings that go on and on for days start looking less like strategy.
- The 8th version of an app or website UX that no one is going to use to buy stuff or enroll now or call your sales team starts looking like bottom priority and fluff
- And that new flashy ad campaign that takes an army of highly and questionably paid consultants months to churn out starts losing its luster to such things as: Smart and quick testing of an informed portfolio of messaging and campaigns that lets the MARKET tell you what's the best message for each demographic
- Digital assets and customer experiences that DRIVE ACTION and new and/or returning customers
- Creative that is brand right and based on data and trends and Cost Per New Sales reports by ad channel, by product line, by customer demographic vs. One Campaign Fits All.

This playbook intends to change the focus on marketing in your mind and in your company. Most importantly, this playbook channels the behaviors, philosophy, and specific tactics to put that new focus into action tomorrow. It's time professional marketers who know how to spend money to drive customer generation help those CEOs and marketing executives in B2B or B2C industries where provable ROI is essential to understand that there is a recipe for success. *There is a marketing plan for B2B and High Value B2C to drive those direct response outcomes in the 21st Century.*

We need to ensure that as long as we're talking about marketing being responsible for ROI, and there is an engine in place to do that daily without fail, that we therefore can have other less data driven conversations, knowing at least someone is not asleep behind the wheel.

Marketing's primary conversation should be about the most immediate, ROI+, and accountable way to get more customers. If you're talking about anything else, then you're doing marketing for a different reason. We've gotten so far away from this as CEOs and as marketers, and I'm certain I know why, speaking as a marketing professional, and it's embarrassing:

- Because it's HARD to profitably drive customers.
- It is TOUGH being accountable for ROI.
- And it's EASY to talk about and be held to SUBJECTIVE measures.

When a CEO who is NOT trained in direct response marketing leans on his or her marketing experts for strategies—both agencies and in-house teams—it's easy for these experts to talk about everything other than the most important thing in marketing.

Customer generation is less of an art and more of a science. It's a daily process using basic math, a mix of tried-and-true digital and traditional marketing methods, and common sense.

But when you start talking about results, you get held to those results and that tends to scare the heck out of anyone who isn't a CEO because it's easy to get fired. Why? Because when there is a quantifiable goal that you either did achieve or did not achieve, the success or failure is black and white and inescapable. And that risk is often terrifying. Heck, you could get fired!

It's easy to keep your job as an agency or as an in-house marketer if it's always someone or something else's fault for a lack of exceptional ROI.

We need to change that.

Marketers should be primarily responsible for the full stack of profitable customer generation.

This book is the battle plan to help CEOs put this conversation into action and make sure it's actually getting done.

WHO THIS BOOK IS *NOT* FOR—LOW PRICE POINT, MASS MARKET B2C

This playbook is not for B2C executives where the net present value (NPV) of a new customer is less than a few hundred bucks, or their B2C product lines would not be considered the luxury good of the category: Coke, Pepsi, fast food restaurants, low cost, high volume consumer package goods companies.

There are already hundreds of books and thousands of agencies in the world that suit the needs and marketplaces of these companies.

This playbook wants to speak to the hundreds of thousands of the forgotten B2B and High Value B2C executives, marketing leaders and anyone doing the real digital work in the trenches. Your types of companies might not be completely forgotten—that's obviously a bit of hyperbole—but the fact is that much less is spoken about successful digital and direct strategies for those types of companies versus mass market B2C or eCommerce.

The CEOs and companies that most marketing books and keynote speakers reach out to in order to win new agency business—the Mass Market B2C world—happens for a reason. These are business environments where it is not fiscally responsible to surgically target each net new consumer, and you don't care about getting one new client. Moreover, these are typically the "whales" in the marketing agency world and the holy grail of agency profit.

So why does this create a world where most marketing experts and agency crosshairs are pointed squarely in the direction of the Mass Market B2C executive?

Because the CEOs and CMOs of these low cost/high volume B2C companies have their hands full deciding on whether to spend more money naming stadiums after grocery store products, or to drop millions of dollars on either a 30- or 60-second spot at the Super Bowl, or get that deal on Rte. 95 billboards near the Walmart exit. They typically have the largest marketing budgets and for the 99 percent of agencies who charge based on a percentage of media, that's pure gold. A conversation about ROI tied directly to the agency's efforts? Those are often either nonexistent or receive the lowest billing in a meeting agenda—which means large margins and profit are not being tied to revenue and Return on Marketing Investment accountability.

The Low Price Point, Mass Market B2C world is the lifeblood of brand advertisers, where the creative emotional play of brand strategy is the only arrow in their marketing quiver.

Too many books have been written by smarter and more successful people than I about creative/brand marketing. There was already one J. Walter Thompson—and there is still very much the incredible Gary Vaynerchuk to lead the world in "building your brand." There is too much pontification about brand strategy at any conference with marketing topics by people using too many buzzwords. Too much content out there with too few tactics to driving short-term/long-term ROI with proven, direct-response, customer generation methods and not enough specifics on how to execute.

I want to change that focus. People running companies and marketing departments need to know that there *are* brass tacks tactics that do, in fact, drive new customers and more revenue. There is a playbook of best practices. While they aren't a magic wand and are not a 100 percent guarantee of overall profitability, they are the things that you need to do at 9:01 am tomorrow, if you're not already doing them.

This is for the silent majority who toil under the yoke of hard outcomes and marketing accountability where X Dollars must = Y Results day after day, quarter after quarter, and who need to get things done in both the short and long term.

This is for the thousands of CEOs and CMOs who need line-by-line ROI in their marketing channel, directly attributable to that activity. This is not about fluffy topics or what we'll call vanity metrics like view-through conversions, likes, and shares on Instagram, and other faux-KPI nonsense.

THE FOCUS AND OUTCOMES

This is your marketing battle plan. That means that the desired outcome of this information is for you to be given the knowledge and real world, no B.S., immediately deployable tactics to have the following:

1. **The strategy and big picture**—answering the WHAT levers and the WHYs for using them—of customer generation focused marketing in the 21st Century.
2. **A best practice checklist** and glossary of ad platforms, marketing and design tactics, and reporting/KPI review that must be done and done correctly every day
3. **The right questions to ask your marketing leadership** to ensure:
   a. they know what they're talking about
   b. they know you know what you're talking about
   c. they are aligned with driving quantifiable marketing results and +ROI, and
   d. you can trust that the baseline essential tactics are being handled properly every day, and that sh*t is getting done.

This is the view from 30,000 feet and 30 feet.

This is for any company in B2C and B2B where driving one new customer is worth paying attention to and reporting upon.

WHAT YOU DON'T WANT TO FOCUS ON

It's equally important to list what reading this book will *not* give you, as every hour of your attention is valuable and finite in supply, so let's list both what we *will* and *will not* cover.

This book will *not* provide nor will it urge you to do the following:

1. High level thoughts about the long-term content strategies and rejoicing the value of brand marketing and purely creative marketing efforts.

    So what will we cover, then, in terms of strategies and marketing goals?

    This playbook is about profitable customer generation tactics today, not brand positioning measured in a net promoter score next year. This is about making this quarter and this year from an EBITDA standpoint. This is about the core engine of tactics driving qualified traffic, enhanced customer contact, and better conversion rates to sale or inquiry. This is about making money and profit and driving new customers at the maximum volume given a budget for the minimum Cost Per Customer Acquisition (CPA). With all rightfully due, genuine respect to Gary V. and other marketing and sales gurus urging long-term plays and patience, there are massively neglected baseline activities that must be done daily or the ship is going to sink before you get to next year. The best pep talk and brand vision cannot fix what is broken and hemorrhaging your money and opportunity cost today. Both are important, but too much is said about branding with general pep talk platitudes and too little about the tactics to win the short game.

    This is about those baseline things. I'll let other people talk about more creative, less direct response, less ROI critical, less ROI certain, more long-term tactics.

    Those marketing efforts *are* valuable, but there are a thousand apostles of that art and too few of the less sexy but more essential religion of X Dollars = Y Results.

2. We will not focus on conversations that are the outcome of executives and marketers sitting in rooms talking about things *other* than ROI. This list of marketing conversations we will not focus on includes but is not limited to:

    a. Topics that don't drive revenue and profit but allow people to hear their own voice, such as:
        i.   The EXACT, perfect phrasing of copy
        ii. The PERFECT image or creative asset
        iii. The BRAND GUIDELINE SACRED COW—the static formula for all things creative—that deprioritizes the customer and prioritizes a fixed message approved by old white men in board rooms (typically)
        iv. The CUSTOMER JOURNEY without using data, heat maps, or site analytics

    No one important gives a damn what messaging or copy or art or creative comes out of a boardroom. Who is the only important person in marketing? The *customer*. Test a wide variety of messages, calls to action, creative, copy, etc. and let the marketplace tell you what works . . . not the other way around.

    I've been doing marketing since I hit the street and now with twenty years, nine figures in ad spend, and a few companies under my belt could be considered to be a marketing expert. And do you know how often my opinion matters or trumps data that shows what the customer responds best to in creative or messaging?

    Never.

    Make a quick and informed decision about where to start in creating banner ads and landing pages and copy for websites but make a *bunch* of stuff you think is intelligent then test it all and get the hell out of the way of the data.

What else are we leaving on the cutting room floor?

b. Feelings and anecdotal garbage that have no place in the 21st Century Direct Response World of Marketing in the trenches.

    Sentences which begin, "So I personally don't use Facebook for business, so it doesn't work" or "I hear our sales team's feedback and they say the leads are" have no place in this century in the boardroom.

c. Buzzwords and activities and cool tech that does not contribute 100 percent to ROI. I want to say this again, COOL, POPULAR, "EVERYONE IS RUNNING IT," SaaS platforms which in reality do nothing more than make CEOs feel like they are doing neat advanced stuff but really do not DEFINITIVELY DRIVE ROI are going to be ignored. They are the cancer of our business world and it is rife with a sickness to spend money on new tech instead of tried, true, and direct levels to drive more customers. No one cares if you feel like you are using the best, newest tech—least of all your balance sheet—if the only ROI is your comfort level and the only KPI achieved is the ability to check the box of what someone else told you was a "game changer."

d. Things that are not 100 percent essential to customer generation in the world of marketing—there are no nice-to-have marketing activities here. The only tactics and activities and strategies here are proven profitable more often than not, use data, and is DIRECTLY responsible for ROI.

And what is the final list of fever-pitch popular marketing topics that we need to deprioritize in your mind and world?

Other incredibly popular, fluffy marketing concepts like "brand engagement," "audience profiling," "decile scoring" and "evergreen content strategies" that you hear well paid keynote speakers shout out as The Shiny New Object of the month might be in the next book. The book after this one, where we make certain your ship is free of efficiency leaks and your direct response customer generation engine is running and accountable. We'll get to the things that sound amazing as a soundbite at a conference but in the world I've lived in and the marketing I consider my occupational religion, tend to be much better on a PowerPoint and less effective as a real tactic.

This book is about creating new or engaging with current customers and driving more revenue and profit, and the methods, tech, ad channels, and work that it takes to do those things all day every day. Sometimes they're not sexy, but they definitively work.

Let's get to it.

CHAPTER 1

THE ESSENTIAL GLOSSARY: THE AD CHANNELS, TERMS, AND TECHNOLOGY USED

STEPHEN HAWKING WROTE THAT "MATHEMATICS IS the language of nature." As a once-upon-a-time crappy physics major who learned in his freshman year that there are people who are actually *good* at physics, I'd instead say the following: **Mathematics is the alphabet of nature; physics is the language.**

And so it is with 21st Century digital marketing. To understand and apply the science you must first learn the alphabet.

You must read and understand everything in this section if you want to foster and manage an effective and profitable digital and direct marketing effort. As such, I would urge you to not skip ahead unless you can buzz through this chapter and nod your head at everything listed.

The less of this you know, the less able you are as an executive to curate and call out bullshit—the two most essential and undervalued skills when building on new ground and striving for a profitable marketing outcome.

You must understand what each element in the marketing quiver does and what it's supposed to do before we talk about what arrow to grab and unleash based on who you are, what industry you're in, etc.

This will be in four incredibly essential topics, covering the things that are the beating heart and driving force that powers digital and direct response digital marketing. This is as essential to walking away with the ability to do real stuff as it is to wear pants to the office every day. We need to review:

1. We need to start defining some core, daily-used digital marketing terms, buzzwords, and acronyms with a brief **glossary**.

2. The **digital advertising channels** that are the main drivers to customer generation.

3. The **type of creative** (words, images, etc.) needed to ensure efficiency in striving for better ROI. Creative = anything a prospective customer sees, like ads or websites or content, which can help or hurt someone taking action. UX/UI (user experience, user interface) is important as well when turning potential customers into customers, but that's for another discussion and is less low hanging fruit/large impact than the other topics covered here.

4. The **types of websites** prospective customers experience as part of a digital and direct marketing strategy. (Hint: it isn't your homepage.)

5. The **data, reporting, and marketing attribution concepts** necessary to know what's really happening to your marketing budget; what specific actions your money is creating and the value of those customer actions.

6. The difference between **proprietary digital advertising** and using **pay per lead ("PPL") affiliates** and if your industry should care. (Hint: most shouldn't; those that do REALLY do.)

But at a high level, we are going to focus on the MUST HAVEs in 21st Century B2B and High Value B2C customer generation across all industries. If you already are a savant at SEM or FB Power Editor (you can't stop me from calling it that) or Google Tag Manager or best-practice Landing Page UX/UI, feel free not to read that part of the appendix when subsequent chapters refer to them.

After you know about each of the tools in the toolkit, we can *then* view all the things to learn and execute based on *your specific needs*, each tending to increase in granularity and digital and direct response acumen as we dive deeper into who you are and what you need. **These will be the chapters in this playbook.**

With both the short and the long term, there are strategies, marketing and analytics team behaviors, and tactics to learn to ensure you're running effective 21st Century customer generation focused marketing. In addition, and more specifically regarding the tactics, there is the deeper need to understand the science, math, terminology, and most importantly the technology used in this brave new world.

But without understanding the terms and technology that underpins and powers every smart decision and every customer targeted and every ROI-focused report we read, you're not armed with the ability to understand those whom you manage and the art and sciences they deploy.

Let's begin with covering the definitions of the core buzzwords and acronyms used every day in the 21st Century world of marketing.

(1) A DIGITAL ADVERTISING GLOSSARY: THE KEY TERMS AND ACRONYMS

ROI—I think I use this acronym more than any other because (a) I'm in marketing, and (b) I think marketing should focus on this more than do most businesspeople. While most professionals use this as a percentage, I use it both as a raw number and as a percentage, depending on the conversation I'm having. So what do I mean?

At a high level, it's a close-enough proxy to gauge if a marketing campaign helped your company make a profit. Technically it's slightly more nuanced, though I'd contend that the high level is good enough for most conversations. But specifically when I say ROI, I mean for the most part a slightly longer acronym: ROMI, or **Return on Marketing Investment**. This is absolutely unique to every company, but is different for every product or service line you offer, every unique physical location or online store you run. But it's a simple piece of math, and let's simplify it using a B2B example (as I'll just use my firm and we're B2B) though the math is only slightly different among the two different audiences in this book: The B2B marketer and the High Value B2C marketer.

In B2B marketing, let's use the example of my company and let's make it very simple. Let's assume that all of our new clients are the same type versus the reality that some clients use us for full stack digital advertising only, while some use us for that *plus* web design and attribution modeling and call center work. But let's assume every client of mine asks for the same thing. And this B2B scenario will be different from a High Value B2C calculation because while the agency costs are about the same, the advertising spends are higher because you're trying to target more humans.

The basic equation as a percentage is: (The Increase in Profit) / (The Cost of Marketing: both the Ad Spend + Agency Fee)

The other way to communicate it is as a raw number: (The Increase in Profit)—(The Cost of Marketing: both the Ad Spend + Agency Fee). This, while not absolutely academically correct, is often used in business conversations far away from accountants and CFOs. It tends to answer the question of "exactly what did I get for all that fancy digital marketing work?"

Here is the example in a basis B2B framework:

And let's assume that every new client gives us $25,000 on average per month in revenue to do our work. So our annual average revenue for each new client is $300,000.

In terms of expenses, let's say that I spend $10,000 per month in Google and Bing, $7,500 per month in Facebook and LinkedIn, and $1,500 in banner ads. That's going to come to $228,000 per year in advertising expenses. Now, I'm lucky that *technically* I don't have to have a line item for an agency to actually do the work, which is significant because, well, we *are* an agency, but let's assume it costs an average of $20,000 per month. That's $240,000.

So the total expenses for the year are $468,000.

To calculate the ROI of our marketing (again, technically what I'm doing is the RO[marketing]I), we do the following tracking and math:

- The $228,000 in ads drove 590 leads. That's $386 per "raw" lead.
- Of those B2B leads, only 10 percent were qualified leads, meaning they were from companies we would consider a good target account, and the contact information was of someone in the ballpark of being a decision maker or an influencer of said decision.
- That means the number of qualified sales leads (QSLs) was 59 and the cost per qualified lead is $3,864.

- And we close on average 10 percent of our QSLs so that is six new accounts.
- And if our average account brings us $300,000, that's an increase of $1,800,000.

Now every conversion point I just used isn't an exact reflection of my business, but it's definitely within the range of a sober B2B sales funnel. Approximately a $400 cost per lead for B2B? It can easily be lower, but let's just go with this as it's a conservative figure. A 10 percent rate of qualified leads to raw leads? Check. The fact that we close one in 10 good leads? That sounds sober as well.

Let's then go deeper and use some standard CFO-level reports to finish the ROI equation example.

If I do $1.8mm in revenue from these efforts, and my average B2B profit margin is 15 percent, then that means that profit I'm making in real dollars is $270,000 more. And in B2B, especially a SaaS business, 15 percent margins are not that impressive. But I'm OK with keeping this example pretty sober.

So the final return on marketing investment (or what we are calling ROI in this book) is:

(The Increase in Profit) / (The Cost of Marketing:
both the Ad Spend + Agency Fee)
($270,000) / ($468,000) = 57.7 percent ROI

In a more colloquial, conversational sense, I'll just say that our ROI for the year was $270,000 because I have that much more in real dollars versus not having done anything at all. But again, that's not academically correct in the accounting sense, but you'll definitely hear it in informal marketing conversations.

So when I say ROI, the high level is that I'm talking about how much, if any, incremental profit your marketing drove taking into account all marketing expenses.

Let's now dive into the real digital marketing key terms and acronyms that you'll hear at every meeting and water cooler conversation on a digital marketing floor.

CPM = One type, and the "OG" version from the mid-1990s, of pricing used in digital advertising, that is still one of the main ways you pay when you run digital ads.

It's short for "**Cost Per Mille**," and *mille* is Latin for thousand, and it means that every time you *see* a thousand of something (like a banner ad), you pay some amount of money. For example, this could be for every time you see one of your ads on Facebook. Or one of your banner ads. The important word for that is "see" which we will get to in a minute. It was the original basis and first type of pricing construct used on the internet. It is important to understand that in the past 5+ years this pricing structure is still aggressively and intelligently used by the most advanced media buyers, but in many cases and in basic and unsophisticated ad campaigns, this pricing structure to an untrained media buyer can be incredibly dangerous. It's the billboard of digital because 100 percent of the risk falls on the advertiser. You pay for someone to SEE something, not DO something. All the risk in the spending of money to get someone to DO something (the ethos, pathos and logos of digital customer generation) is on your shoulders. But in the right hands with sophisticated media teams, techniques, and ad platforms, this can unleash greatness. However, this is *not* the same as paying a flat CPM with your regional newspaper's "digital ad team" to put your ads on local websites. That's setting money on fire and the CPM is the culprit with those frankly dumb media buys. We'll explain more on that when we talk about the nuances of smart display (also called "banner") advertising.

The bottom line is that for experienced, advanced digital media buyers, buying advertising on a cost per mille basis is actually the standard. Nearly all of our social media and display advertising business is conducted on a CPM basis, so it certainly isn't to say that

CPM pricing is bad but the following methods are better. But cost per thousand pricing structures in the wrong hands can wreak havoc. And it is far more complicated in advanced digital media shops: most of the successful campaigns and ad sets on Facebook are technically CPM, but you can set CPC/CPL targets . . . yet you actually get charged on a CPM basis. But that's beyond the scope of this book.

What you need to know is that CPM was the first type of pricing for online advertising and, in exactly the same way as traditional advertising—such as TV, print, radio, and outdoor—absolutely 100 percent of the risk is on you, the advertiser, because you are paying money for people to see your ad versus actually doing something, like visiting your website, submitting a lead, or making a phone call.

CPC = Cost Per Click. Sometimes called PPC = Pay Per Click.

The very thing that was the birth of what we all know as the promise and glory of digital advertising and ROI-driven marketing. More importantly, it is the "something" that we referred to above when defining CPM pricing—the action that makes the publisher (i.e.: the place where we spend money in advertising) share risk with the advertiser (i.e.: you).

I'm going to swing hard here with the hyperbole, and it's nearly true: the creation of the CPC pricing construct in digital advertising is the equivalent to the resurrection of Christ in the Bible. This changed everything when Google (actually, a search engine ad platform called Overture . . . but that's ancient history) told the world that they'd show your ad a trillion times to a trillion people, but you'll only pay when someone clicks on an ad. A miracle! For the first time in history in advertising, someone selling something to you, the client, was willing to take *some* risk for a good outcome for you! Hallelujah!

Let me say that again: The CPC pricing construct, launched at scale by Google (yes . . . it did exist before, but at a lower critical mass) in 2000, was the first time in the history of marketing where an advertising platform was willing to share some of the sales risk with the advertiser and not absolve themselves of partial ownership and accountability of customer generation (*see*: all traditional media, forever).

This basically is one of the reasons why everyone in digital marketing has a job and why traditional media is going extinct/getting cheaper and why the sun will rise tomorrow. It was the match that lit the bonfire of interest in and acceleration of advertising online.

CPL = Cost Per Lead. A mid-funnel key performance indicator ("KPI" = A data point you want to focus on and make sure you optimize around). The cost, on average, that your media is driving to create a new lead. A lead can be something simple, like a new email address asking for a case study, or discount code to be emailed, and can be as robust as a full record of a human with dozens of data points and full contact information.

PPL = It stands for **Pay Per Lead**, which is both a marketplace and a pricing model to buy the contact information for prospective customers; the companies and industry is also known as Affiliate Markets or Affiliates. These markets are their own genre of media where you can buy these records and consumer data as a commodity, and receive traditionally, on a monthly basis via standard purchase orders.

We're getting into some niche industries here, as this pricing model is only found in economic systems where the supply and demand curves of the marketplace for new customers is so whacked out of reality and is so hyperbolic and aggressive (I'm looking at your for-profit EDU, mortgage, insurance verticals) that you've got businesses that don't do anything other than sell people's information. And Cost Per Lead is the pricing construct for these industries and marketplaces. In this world, the majority of the risk is NOT on the advertiser or client but on the company that spends dollars in either a CPM or CPC world (buying impressions or buying clicks) and tries to turn the stuff into a lead to sell. And since it's risky, they take quite a bit of profit on the top end for those efforts. This environment is incredibly dangerous for any marketing team and company to engage in if you're not skilled and deeply involved in affiliate markets. This is Mos Eisley. This is the greatest collection of scum and villainy in the marketing galaxy. Well, there are some brilliant and amazingly good people in PPL, to be sure, but let's not pretend it's chock full.

How do I know about what lies behind the green curtain of PPL? I used to own an affiliate/PPL (or simply called a "lead gen") company from 2010 to 2017, and worked on the client side buying tens of millions of dollars of leads on a PPL basis. I'm one of the very few who have been on both sides at the senior level. If you're reading this and you don't know what your affiliate strategy is, or if your company has fewer than 10 affiliates in its portfolio, or if you're not actively managing this channel and each PPL vendor to a very specific and tight Cost Per Sale/Enrollment/New Client KPI, stop immediately and seek professional help from an agency that does not up-charge on every lead and that is 100 percent transparent.

But for the majority of people reading this book, you'll never experience this world. May the odds be ever in your favor.*

(* said with love in my heart for the few, amazing and brilliant and awesome humans doing great things in lead gen. . . you know who you are).

PPC—Stands for **Pay Per Click**. It incorrectly refers to paid search engine advertising and, instead, is technically a term for a way to pay for digital media on, you guessed it, a per-click basis.

Second only to the acronym "SEO," this is the most incorrectly used term in marketing. People use PPC to refer to digital advertising on search engines. This is incredibly, inexplicably wrong. It blows my mind how we as professional marketers not only let this stupidity happen, but we encourage it by not correcting laymen.

Again, Pay Per Click is a pricing model, not a digital ad channel like Google or Bing. You don't define an advertising channel by the method they use to charge you. That's like calling retail stores "Buy One Get One" stores because sometimes you can buy stuff like that.

It's wrong and it drives me crazy.

PPC means the way you can pay for some types of advertising. It's 100 percent synonymous with CPC (Cost Per Click). It's the same thing.

You pay some amount of money when someone clicks on your ad.

Let me beat the dead horse because this trend of misusing the acronym PPC has got to stop in digital marketing:

- **CPC** (Cost Per Click) = **PPC** (Pay Per Click). It's ostensibly the same thing in practice (yes, I understand you can back out a CPC by dividing dollars spent by clicks on a CPM basis . . . but that's just splitting hairs the wrong way). The bottom line is that PPC is a pricing structure in the world of digital advertising.
- **PPC does not mean advertising on search engines.**
- **Marketing professionals: Stop misusing this term.**
- **Digital agencies: Stop mis-educating your clients** by using this term to describe what you do when you should know the difference. It's like a PhD in English dropping "irregardless" into the title of the thesis. It's just wrong and is like fingernails on the chalkboard to a well-educated digital professional.

So that's the perfect segue into what *do* people mean when they misuse the acronym PPC? Keep reading!

SEM, also called "Paid Search" = **Paid Search Engine Marketing** (reviewed in depth below). The act of paying for ads on Google, Bing, Yahoo and other search engines. *This is not SEO.* This is different. This is a legitimate, scalable, awesome and data-driven tactic that is the cornerstone to 21st Century Marketing in ninety-nine out of 100 industries and products.

SEM is what people mean when they incorrectly say "PPC."
SEO or **ORGANIC SEARCH** = **Search Engine Optimization** (reviewed a bit in the section below) is the act of doing stuff on your website and pushing content into the ether of the internet in an often-bad ROI attempt to try and convince search engines to "rank you high" for a handful of keywords. This is sold as snake oil 90 percent of the time, and it's a huge problem because the majority of non-marketing executives think it's a scalable and quantitatively certain exercise that belongs at the very top of digital marketing to-do lists. It's not. SEO is neither scalable nor able to be guaranteed via a testing baseline like SEM. This means that, up until a point of diminishing returns, if you spend $1,000 on SEM and get 10 leads and 2 sales, that $100 cost per lead and $500 cost per sale is likely to be what you're going to get when you spend $4,000 or $10,000 in SEM. This is especially true for companies that have nationwide or global products and less true (because of a lower point of diminishing returns) for brick and mortar based companies in rural areas.

So unlike SEM, SEO is not scalable nor is a marketing agency's tactics for SEO very likely to work if they stick to the best practices. But this does not mean all SEO is bad or all marketing companies offering it are selling garbage.

I am, however, yelling from the mountaintops that a lot of smaller companies that sell SEO services do a bad job: they over-sell what SEO can do ("it's free magic!"), and clients are often unaware of where investing in SEO should fit in their marketing plan.

BOTTOM LINE ON SEO:

- SEO is important and good when done correctly. However, I have seen more often than not fellow CEOs and clients spending tens of thousands of dollars on SEO before doing the Core Four digital marketing tactics in this book, and then being incredibly disappointed.

- **You should eventually invest in SEO, but do it long after you deploy everything in this book to drive more leads and customers with quantifiable, scalable, optimizable digital campaigns that have predicable cost per lead and cost per sale KPIs.** Moreover, you should only go with a company for SEO that can offer quantifiable results with a company similar to yours and where you can call a senior person at that company and confirm 100 percent that their SEO was responsible for their happiness.
- Bad SEO is responsible for billions of dollars of wasted time and money and, like the Keyser Söze of marketing, is the greatest trick the devil ever pulled when in the hands of bad marketers. Keep in mind that I'm saying this, and my agency offers SEO as a service. So if that doesn't highlight my warning, nothing will. Again, this is covered in depth below in the search engine section.

Paid Social vs. Organic Social = There are two kinds of advertising messages in the world of Facebook, the most powerful and profitable social network for advertisers. Paid Social can reach billions of people, is surgical, scalable, and has a massive portfolio of targeting tactics and ad units. It's the lever used by professional marketers to drive net new sales and ROI. Organic Social is stuff you post on your company's Facebook page to maintain a nice relationship with current fans. Paid Social and Organic Social are completely different. One can often be done well in-house, without an agency (Organic Social). The other (Paid Social) should be done by weapons-grade digital advertising professionals, nearly always mid to large size digital-first agencies unless you're a Fortune 1000 company with 25-plus digital marketers in your marketing department. Similar to the reach limitations and desired outcome certainty of SEO, Organic Social is more of a content and current client strategy than a customer generation tactic.

BOTTOM LINE =

- **Paid Social** = Paying money for very robust types of image and video based ads where you can target any user in the entire social platform (so, 2-plus billion FB users) and target them using incredibly advanced ads serving logic and demo/psychographic filters. This gives you weapons-grade ability to advertise to people who have no idea who you or your company are. Driving traffic, often, to landing pages and websites you control (vs. your company's organic page inside the social network) allows you to be much more able to make the person DO something.

- **Organic Social** = Showing your content and basic advertising messages to your existing audience and to only those whom have "liked" your page. Free to an extent, but often limited in terms of percentage of your existing fans unless you pay, and incapable of driving traffic outside of the social network, thereby limiting your ability to make the person DO something that drives sales in an efficient manner.

Don't confuse Paid with Organic Social. Ninety percent of professional client side marketers do, and think just because someone in their company is posting stuff on their company's organic page, that they are "doing social marketing."

If you're only running Organic, you're not really "doing social advertising."

(2) A DIGITAL ADVERTISING GLOSSARY: THE ESSENTIAL DIGITAL ADVERTISING CHANNELS

The following digital advertising platforms are the main drivers of not only digital customer generation, but the cornerstone of all advertising efforts, both traditional and digital. We will dive into effective traditional tactics in future chapters, but (a) these are your cornerstones to any marketing in any industry, and (b) the hardest to understand and deploy well.

There are four ways humans are advertised "at" digitally. That's it. If you know what these can do, what they can't do, and what products, services, customer types, and industries each is ideal for (or where they're weak), then you're a well-informed quarterback of 21st Century digital marketing. That's not to say that direct marketing isn't difficult to do well, but we're not going to review what a call center does or what direct mail looks like. We will talk about nuances for each of these channels, and how they partner with best practice digital advertising tactics, but for now, let's dive into the four digital channels:

- Search Engines
- Social Networks
- Display Advertising
- Email Campaigns

Yes, there are more niche categories of digital advertising, such as audio ads run on Pandora or the upcoming brave new world of the Amazon Echo's and Siri's of the world. But those are the future. Let's talk about the present best practices and the four key digital ad platforms.

SEARCH ENGINES

There are many out there in the world, and even a few in the US that fly under the radar (I'm looking at you, www.Ask.com), but there is the core group of three (Google, Bing, and Oath/Yahoo!) you need to focus on to ensure you are keying in on the essential pieces in digital advertising for High Value B2C and B2B customer generation.

There is a ton of misinformation out there when non-digital marketing experts talk about search engines, and here are some bullet points to clear things up (we did cover it above in the definitions section, but it's important enough to mention again):

PPC stands for Pay Per Click, not paid search engine marketing. PPC is a pricing model, meaning it's a common way marketers pay to use some ad platforms, but here are the problems with that:

1. A pricing model isn't an advertising channel, it's just one way you can pay for stuff.
2. Other advertising channels can operate on a Pay Per Click (PPC) basis . . . like display networks and social media.
3. Saying PPC can mean advertising on any ad channel that allows you to buy media per click.

This drives me crazy.

PPC does not mean Paid Search Engine Marketing, but a majority of business professionals incorrectly use it this way, so beware of this in conversation. But that error pales in comparison to the next point.

The most wicked and dangerous dual misconception in all of digital advertising is the following problem . . . and I guarantee that you are current working with people who are committing this atrocity—even fairly smart people who call themselves digital advertising professionals. *If you read and take away only one thing from this book, this could be it:*

SEO is *not* SEM, and SEO is *not* your solution to drive more customers in a pull-a-lever, scalable tactic with highly predictable outcomes. Moreover, SEO is sold like snake oil more often that you would believe by under-skilled marketers who only want to take thousands of your dollars per month and give you unquantifiable activities that often can and should be done better inside your company.

This is going to take a while to unpack, and that was a bit more rant-level than ideal for a nonfiction business book, but I promise these are the greatest misconceptions in the world of digital marketing. They bleed many companies of their budget, destroying any trust and faith that clients have of the potential for smart and accountable digital marketing, and doing a massive disservice to the men and women who do real, data-driven, multi-channel digital and direct marketing.

Here is the high level of the difference:

1. SEO and SEM, roughly speaking, represent the two different types of things you see on a Google or Bing or Yahoo search engine results page.
2. SEM (**"Search Engine Marketing"**) is the practice of bidding on the right term to show up on the results page—based on thousands and thousands of unique keywords relevant to your product or service—and you pay only when someone clicks on your ad.
3. SEO (**"Search Engine Optimization"**) has nothing to do with a paid media strategy. This is the practice of creating good content surrounding a handful of keywords—not hundreds or thousands—and hoping that Google, Bing, or Yahoo bless you with the authority for those keywords, and therefore a higher rank on the results page.

Here are the facts, misconceptions and problems:

1. Good, ethical (what we call "white hat") SEO is an important part of every company's long-term marketing strategy.

Let me start there, and say it again: SEO is important.

2. However, it is rarely if ever one of the first half dozen things you must do when creating your company's digital marketing strategy and presence.

3. One of the main problems is that SEO is sold as free magic, where for a few (or many) thousands of dollars per month (so . . . not free), someone will create content and push it out into the ether (onsite vs. offsite SEO, as it is called) and get other websites and portals to take notice, link back to your main website, and do a few other neat things with viral

infographics (or other buzzwords) and KAPOW! You have magically been given good first page results right below the paid ads by Google.

4. More specifically, there are massive, business-damaging problems with SEO, not because of what it can do, but how it is sold to companies like yours and what people promise it will do.

   a. You cannot be certain it will ever work because you cannot tell Google what to do. Many companies spend tens of thousands of dollars and get nothing for it. Often they get even less return if they hire a smaller SEO-only company that also wants to re-design their website.

   b. You cannot control the web page the viewer is sent to vs. the keyword you are ranked for. This is unfortunate, and often the page in question is on your main marketing website with crappy direct response UX/UI, and any traffic will convert poorly to a lead and customer. We will get into the massive problem between your main website vs. landing pages . . . and why your website should rarely be the recipient of traffic you intend to convert to a lead and sale. But with SEO, you're not able to tell Google to drive the traffic to a landing page.

   c. It completely removes your power to send humans to your ultimate weapon in converting visitors into customers: the landing page. But we will cover that much more in-depth in future chapters.

   d. It takes six or more months to see results . . . and those results come less from quantifiable and measurable activities and more from what is done in the paid search engine marketing (SEM) world

   e. SEO is not a lever to pull and is not linearly scalable. Meaning, just because you have a list of 100 keywords/

phrases you'd like to rank well for, does not mean that because it took four months and $20,000 of some SEO agency's fees to get you ranked for three keywords, then for an additional three keywords, you'll get the same results.

f. Unless you have a massive, multi-million-dollar marketing budget and are already doing every low hanging Phase I/Day 1 tactic in this book, you're not going to be able to use SEO to get your website ranked for more than ten keywords. So if you sell a few products or a few different services, you're very limited in what your SEO investment can cover.

And if after all this, there is still one person reading this that has any atom in their body not aware of the marketing danger of confusing SEO with SEM, let me use a personal example: My agency offers and sells white-hat, content driven SEO services and I still do not recommend that companies at the beginning of their "Phase 1, We're New To Online Advertising" journey invest in this before they ensure that the other dozen proven, profitable tactics are being employed.

- **SEO is a nice-to-have not a need-to-have** for every single business which does not have the basics of digital advertising already set up, running (The Phase I in this Playbook, to be reviewed in this book) and showing good results.
- **SEO is not a magic lever to drive new business.** It is a long-term play with a giant question mark of efficacy and an even bigger question mark of definitive results.
- **SEO is a terrible choice if you need a scalable lever**, with predicable results, to drive more customers.
- **SEO is a good choice** for those companies already doing all of the things in this book, have a reliable sales pipeline established, and who understand their mid-funnel and ultimate KPIs and

what each paid digital channel is contributing to their bottom line. In short: SEO is a great set of tactics for companies already doing a good job with the essential elements of 21st Century Marketing. But the reason for this book is that the vast majority of companies—and likely including yours— aren't doing that and, therefore, are spending money on SEO too early. It is a horrendous waste that duplicitous marketers take advantage of hundreds of thousands of times each year.

Of the hundreds of companies I've worked with and/or have insight into their marketing operations, not one needed SEO services on Day 1. None. ZERO.

So don't be tricked—as many corporations are—into buying SEO services that are either (a) vapor-ware, or (b) far too early in their priority list to be as impactful as other tactics. SEO, like good web design, is more about good housekeeping and creating desirable, quality content and planning for long-term traction around a few essential keywords where your company actually has a thought leadership presence.

And because so many smaller, SEO-only shops are doing poor work and preying on the 90 percent of executives and clients who don't know the difference between SEO and SEM, I'm even more reluctant to recommend jumping into SEO.

SEO is important if managed by the right professionals, but you need to prioritize it properly and be aware of its limitations.

And if you're one of the people hawking SEO services and (a) not explaining the difference between SEO and SEM clearly to your prospective clients, (b) not mitigating their expectations for what SEO can do and in what period of time, (c) promising "first page results," and (d) not urging the client to see their marketing as a portfolio of interrelated activities that need to be prioritized by high impact and low hanging fruit vs. SEO as a silver bullet, *please stop.* What you are selling might have made sense in 2005, but not now. It complicates the lives of legitimate digital marketers and our clients.

SEO is no longer one of the first half dozen things that any High Value B2C and B2B company needs.

KEY SEM BEST PRACTICES:

While there are differences in the type of device a human uses (e.g.: mobile vs. desktop) to run a search, this is the share of market that each of the main search engines have (data from Statista, Inc.) from a recent report by an independent third party using a simple 10-year trend to show remarkable stability in the search market.

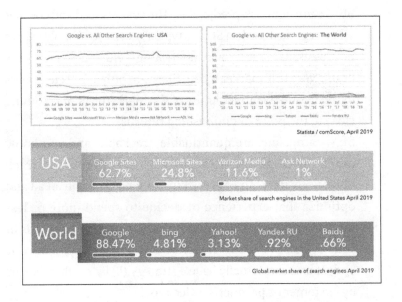

So, for the majority of High Value B2C and B2B enterprises, we'll focus on building scalable, highly-indexed-to-be-ROI-positive SEM campaigns on Google, Bing (Microsoft), and Yahoo (which will eventually disappear beyond 2020).

Keep in mind that when the chart above says "sites," that is because Google and Bing power and are the underlying tech on many large portals that are white-labeled. So even if you're not on Google.com, you still may be using Google when you enter words into a search bar on a large portal.

Lastly, and because we care about tactics that are highly correlated with successful customer generation, this is why we are focusing on SEM versus SEO:

- SEM campaigns are scalable, and for national campaigns (meaning you are selling goods or services across the USA) they typically have a high ceiling before you hit the point of diminishing returns and start seeing a hockey stick exponential increase in your Cost Per Sale/Cost Per Lead. We like things that can scale at a flat or a linear rate as you spend more money.

- SEM campaigns are predictable. The cost per lead and cost per sale you got last week in SEM is typically what you should expect next week, as long as you're not testing—either geographically or in a very tiny market where there are only 1,000 customers in the USA—the upper limits of the marketplace and coming close to the point of diminishing returns

- SEM campaigns are quantifiable, trackable, and you know exactly what happens to every $1 spent. You can track obsessively the path of every human who clicks on an ad and optimize that experience or decide to spend more or less money on the exact ad group (the sub-cluster of keywords in your overall portfolio). This means you have control of your budget and can actually have a strategy (!!) by product line or by customer or product/service type!

- SEM campaigns are optimizable. This means that you're going to have dozens of smaller SEM campaigns that make up your whole SEM portfolio and each of those will have a different cost per sale. You, as the client, should know what your goals are, what your needs are by product or by service or by client type, and you can decide if, how, when, and why to invest more into that line item for your business. SEM is a lever for net new customer generation.

- SEM is often, not always, the best channel—digital or direct—in the world for new customers when you take into account the volume and cost per sale or cost per new customer acquisition. To quote one my senior digital expert at Level Agency, "It's the best permission you're ever going to get" in the world of advertising . . . ." Not only are they a relevant audience, but they're actively thinking about "your product or service." So let me say this again, because it's a big deal: nine times out of ten, for High Value B2C and B2B there is no better volume driver on earth at great (low) cost per customer acquisitions than SEM. Period.

We will cover this in later chapters, but if you're not running baseline SEM campaigns (e.g.: Tradename search on your brand), you are doing marketing wrong in 2020 and will do so in the future.

SEARCH ENGINES BEYOND 2020

The biggest change from the first two decades of search engine marketing and what will be the third decade of the most transformative advertising opportunity since the invention of the television will be tactics that allow Google and Bing to reach your prospective customers before they type something into a search field. This is what is called going "up-funnel."

Google has already launched ad units and tactics that will allow their ad platform to let advertisers show relevant visual ads—videos and images—to targeted prospective customers without those customers Googling those keyword phrases that we all bid on today. Whether it's knowing if someone has visited your website, submitted a lead and provided their email address, or has Googled some more broad phrase relevant to your company or product, Google has been offering those up-funnel, pre-Google-your-exact-keyword for some time. Now, with the use of machine learning and the fact that most people are logged into their Google account, and Google has data on who these people are and what they've queried, they can show visual ads to those individuals *before* they search. For now, those ad units are called Discovery Ads, and the use of images and video (eventually) for your search engine results are here. They will only get more aggressive at competing directly against what was the domain of social networks (the best places to target the right people with visual and rich media ads without them doing anything) which means that Google and eventually Bing will no longer just be the place to spend money at the bottom of the customer lead generation funnel.

SOCIAL NETWORKS

There are many out there, and every six to twelve months the world of digital advertising is introduced to the following:

- New networks in their infancy with promise for marketers
- Existing, popular community networks that might get their act together and provide what we need as ROI-focused advertisers (Pinterest, Snapchat, LinkedIn . . . albeit slowly)
- The leading platforms that lie at the heart of 100 percent of all of our direct response advertising and which change their interfaces and give us anxiety attacks (Facebook and Instagram)
- Newer social-ish networks (or whatever they're going to be called in 2025) that focus on one topic, have some community aspects, and might be able to be weaponized for direct response marketing in the future with good ROI (Alexa/any voice-command platform, Pandora, or Spotify, in-game or in-app ads, any of the voice-driven technologies and solutions out there)

FACEBOOK AND INSTAGRAM:

Simply put, Facebook's advertising platform, which also powers its sister social network Instagram, is the best thing since Google AdWords for advertising, which itself was the best thing for advertising since parchment paper nailed to church doors, or spoken language in word of mouth.

If you or your company—and I don't care what product or service you offer—aren't using this platform, I guarantee that things are in very bad shape in your world. I don't care if you make spatulas, Ferraris, 20-ton earth movers, or toothpicks, or if your service offering is global consulting or you invented a SaaS platform that talks to sheep: Facebook is as essential to your marketing success in generating customers. It's as critical as your website or the telephone your sales team uses to communicate with the world. Put this nearly as close to the top of the list as Tradename SEM, discussed above.

Facebook is that good, it's that powerful and it's that profitable.

Most importantly, the type of advertising I advocated here is *not* "getting likes on Facebook." Similar to SEO in how frequently it is completely misunderstood and confused with real direct response, paid digital advertising is, in the realm of customer generation, fairly worthless. That type of advertising *outcome*, if I could call "Likes" an outcome, has little measurable value. If it does have any value, it's as a low-on-the-ladder peg on the customer journey that is the social network equivalent of opening the SkyMall catalog on an airplane. Sure, we've all done it. But most of the time it's a quick reaction to a fleeting moment (cool photo in your Facebook feed, the flight attendant yelled at you for still having your cell phone on, etc.).

We will not discuss the actual ad units and specific Facebook and Instagram tactics to deploy in this section (that's covered in Playbook sections in future chapters), but we must explain how Facebook targets viewers and give some examples of what it can do.

While we're not going to get into the ad units and user experiences you can build (Chapters 3 and 4), it is important to mention that Facebook is the #2—and often #1—driver of new customers. This depends on your industry, but good digital advertisers on Facebook are able to drive incredibly competitive (i.e.: low) Cost Per Acquisitions because of how unique and robust and flat-out-awesome Facebook's ad experiences are and how much these ads can *convey via video and text* to the audience. As a quick example, both the carousel and collection ad units on Facebook are amazing for a fifteen- to twenty-second video pitch with great direct response lead and customer generation KPIs. So it's not just about the targeting: it's also about the fact that you can explain your company's value proposition with video and amazing creative assets and use those precious seconds of attention to explain why a customer should click and buy.

Every week I hear from an executive that "they tried Facebook and aren't seeing good results so it doesn't work." I can say with near certainty, and certainly in the High Value B2C world (higher education, financial services, expensive consumer products in particular), that they are flat out wrong and the only reason Facebook didn't work is because the people they hired to do it were terrible. And instead of understanding what on a national and global basis is being proven day after day with real data and results is borderline fact, they throw their hands up and walk away from the channel entirely.

"We've tried nothing and are all out of ideas." I hear it every week. I urge you to be brave enough to understand that nine times out of ten, it's because you didn't have the right people doing the digital advertising and not "because Facebook doesn't work."

Let's first briefly walk through the business reasons of why social networks are so important in customer generation for your company. Consider the customer journey (visuals below) of a person completely unaware that they need *anything*, let alone that they know about your company, to the point of sale where they become a faithful new customer in your CRM. The only digital channels where you can compete for new customers before they start actively shopping—what we call going **"up-funnel"** or **prospecting**, which is to say the world and mind of a new customer before they Google something—is in the realm of social networks and banner ads.

Remember, offline advertising has been empirically proven to be a trash-can-fire-in-a-prison-cell bad for ROI with often ten times the cost per acquisitions for new customers, even if these old school channels were well priced, which they are *not*. Using these channels, you can't track your customers well, you can't surgically optimize your efforts, and you are marketing in the dark. Now, if traditional advertising was priced at one tenth of its current cost, and ROI is the goal shown via the data point of low cost per customer acquisition, then my opinion of the value of traditional media would change. But even that will never change the inherent limitations of tracking, targeting, and optimization.

So the advertising channels where you must compete up-funnel are banner ads and social networks. Buying email lists from brokers is a joke and was effective in 2003 but is not in the new world. Google and Bing (and formerly Yahoo!, but that search engine has been fully folded into Bing and likely their ad platform will disappear by the time you read this) have massive competition . . . heck, my mom probably has a Google Ads account. And, again, offline vehicles driving marketing is like shooting darts blindfolded in a loud bar after too many expensive Patron shots.

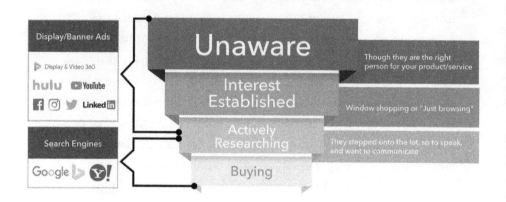

Customer Journey + Ad Channels and Platforms

And between banner ads and social networks, the targeting—the ability to put the right ad in front of the right person at the right time—is an order of magnitude better, especially with Facebook and Instagram, than even the best DSP* display media buy. (*DSP, again, is a fancy marketing term for buying banner impressions on something akin to the NASDAQ with a *decent* idea of whose eyeballs belong to each impression.)

So, social networks are THE best way to reach your audience with killer, best-in-marketing creative ad units (we'll talk about that more in Chapter 4), so target them surgically with the best demographic/psychographic data points known to mankind for a good price!

Let me show you some of the targeting possibilities that Facebook can provide, and this is only a fraction of what it can do. I'll use two platforms:

- A High Value B2C campaign (i.e., more niche, affluent individuals)
- A B2B campaign that I run for my own agency (a service-based B2B where I want my sales team to talk to decision makers and those with access to purse strings).

But this is an example of the types of targeting you can use . . . it's borderline inexplicable and magic to many people—just watch a clip of Mark Zuckerberg testifying in front of the US Senate in 2018 explaining that they sell ads, or the CEO of Google that same year reminding a senator that Google doesn't make the iPhone.

These platforms are simply the best thing to happen to digital advertising and your company's marketing and customer generation since the telephone in 1876, and Google AdWords' Pay Per Click pricing model and ad platform in 2000.

HIGH VALUE B2C FACEBOOK TARGETING EXAMPLE:

Let's say I want to target the following humans, and believe me this is just scratching the surface of what Facebook can do:

- Female
- Lives in the Chicago DMA
- Is middle income/upper-middle income
- Moderately well-educated
- And a mom with teenagers+
- One child
- Married

Example of one of many, many niche customer-profiles you can build on Facebook and an example of how to do it:

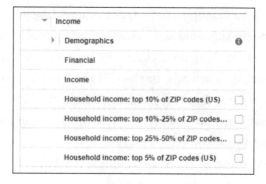

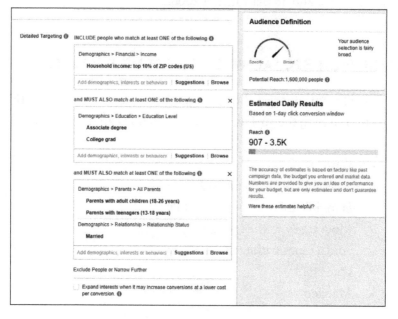

- This shows a few of the types of financial and professional targeting filters you can use (as of 2019/early 2020 as these things change quickly):
  - ° Household income
  - ° Name of company a person works for, if the company is big enough
- Job title via third-party data like Oracle (some are still in the FB platform)
- Home ownership and type

- Education level, as well as college or grad school affiliation or degree type or program of interest
- We then move to one of the dozens of family composition filters you can use:
  ○ Are you a mom?
  ○ Core "interest" targeting based on general hobby/lifestyle categories and anything people have raised their hand and have said "I love this Facebook page about woodworking or cars or ballet"
  ○ Relationship status: Married, single, divorced, etc.

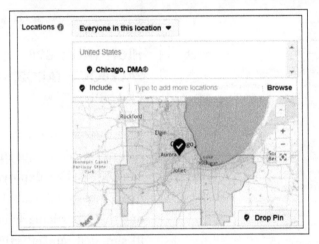

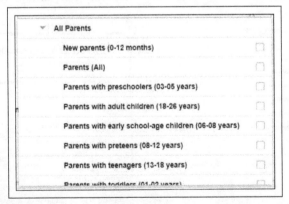

Then you would deploy rich media/video ads with unique words and calls to action across the numerous types of Facebook ad units (we'll review later) to each of these carefully targeted groups of people. And trust me when I say that the examples above just scratch the surface of the types of targeting Facebook and Instagram can weaponize. If you know how to use the platform, it's amazingly powerful and profitable.

One of the most powerful targeting features (as mentioned above) for B2B, job title targeting, has come in and out of the Facebook ad platform a few times. So it is essential to understand that each of these ad platforms, and social media in particular, changes literally every three to six months. You must keep abreast of what they actually offer to drive the best ROI and results.

HIGH VALUE B2B FACEBOOK TARGETING EXAMPLE:

Choosing from the hundreds of B2B lead generation campaigns I've deployed for my company, I'll walk through one that I particularly love for its simplicity and effectiveness:

LIMITATIONS OF LINKEDIN—THE #1 ELEPHANT IN EVERY B2B MARKETING CONVERSATION

When writing anything about this industry—or thinking you know something beyond the shadow of a hint of doubt—you need to always assume things can change every month, and that in ninety days, your proclamations could turn to embarrassing heresy. You hear this a lot from other industries and skill sets and, for the most part, it's bullshit.

Not that much changes in accounting other than tax law, occasionally. Or sales. Or Widget Industry X. Or whatever. "Things are moving at light speed" . . . that cliché blanket statement found in billions of Powerpoints and keynote speeches, is pretty darn worthless.

But not in this vertical.

Let me show you why this is actually true in digital marketing, and how wrong I would have been if my team and I hadn't bled and hustled and worked to be on the leading edge of digital advertising. Because I could have looked like an idiot and you would not have received solid guidance.

HERE IS WHAT I *WAS* GOING TO SAY ABOUT LINKEDIN, UNTIL Q4 OF 2018:

In eight out of ten meetings with executives, particularly in the B2B space and luxury good B2C space, the first social network that non-experts suggest that my agency test (or assume my agency will be using) as the core of our paid social network media strategy is LinkedIn.

And I have to tell them that there is likely no way that we'll spend more than a few percentage points of their media on LinkedIn. Why? Because every year and quarter since I've been able to run paid ads on LinkedIn, it has not been an

ROI-friendly customer generation and direct response digital channel. Maybe great for branding, but not great at turning dollars into leads.

Didn't expect that, right? "But LinkedIn is for business and no one uses Facebook for business," Right?

But data and real-world experience doesn't lie. So this requires some explanation.

Our agency has been actively deploying paid advertisements for a number of customers on LinkedIn for over six years and I've personally tried to work with it as a direct response customer or lead generation ad channel for longer than that. Without question, the lead and customer generation-focused capabilities and results of this platform are far inferior to the results our digital marketing experts are deriving from Facebook, Google, Bing, and Yahoo.

Let me be even more direct: If someone tells you that LinkedIn is a better direct response platform for Money In => Leads and Customers Out, they are either (a) lying to you, or (b) have no idea what they are talking about in best practice direct response digital.

Keep in mind, I so badly want LinkedIn to get its act together that it hurts. I am the biggest advocate—and have literally begged our reps and any relationships I have with current and former LinkedIn employees—for them becoming a channel worthy of spending budget at scale for direct response. Let me re-emphasize this: I have personally had multiple, direct conversations with everyone from junior account reps to senior executives on the product side at LinkedIn borderline begging them to steal every single one of Facebook's advertising platform levers, from the types of rich media-driven ads to the amazingly robust and granular ad targeting to the deep, immersive ad units that come in dozens of visual permutations.

Do you think I like being handcuffed with only two main digital ad channels (Google and Facebook) to spend large budgets within? Do you think that, as a professional marketer and executive, that I care where a good customer comes from?

I don't, in both cases.

But the LinkedIn platform has not responded with anything but aggressive disinterest at building an advertising platform where we as ROI-driven marketers can find a good home for your budgets. They're simply not ready to be worthy of your investment.

So, until LinkedIn starts paying attention to and solving for the gaping holes (listed below) that are the primary cause for its distant third tier status, we recommend that only the clients we serve with the deepest of pockets and budgets for "future potential" or "up-funnel" test ad channels invest.

HERE IS WHAT I AM NOW GOING TO SAY ABOUT LINKEDIN TODAY:

1. I was wrong or, rather, could be wrong in 2020 and beyond in terms of LinkedIn being flat-out bad for direct response digital advertising and cost-effective lead and customer generation.

2. A few months after I wrote the words above, LinkedIn started to drive the beginnings of what could be a massive, profitable, direct-response friendly ad channel for advertisers and agencies. Things changed and I was lucky enough to follow the core mantra of good digital marketing which is "test, test, then test again."

3. Because we are good stewards of our clients' money (and being smart and good means testing everything, even things that you are pretty sure are not going to work because they didn't work last month and the 100 months before that), we tested LinkedIn for a High Value B2C campaign where we

know that industry cold.

4. We worked with what I'll call a Seal Team 6 of Give-a-Damn-ability at LinkedIn that took over one of the industries we focus on (often ad platforms have industry-specific account teams, and LinkedIn is no different).

5. This team was different. And most importantly, LinkedIn was changing and enhancing their paid advertising technology.

6. And while it's still early in testing and the jury is still out, my feelings about LinkedIn (which have been 100 percent defensible for five to seven years since I've been trying to spend my clients' money on that platform) have changed because the platform actually produced a good direct-response result and, in terms of mid-funnel KPIs, went head to head with Facebook.

So, again, it's not nearly a home run yet for B2B or High Value B2C direct-response marketing and it's not as if I'm going to suggest that you re-appropriate 25 percent of your total digital budget to LinkedIn. That being said, things from a performance and opportunity standpoint are absolutely better Quarter over Quarter and definitely Year over Year for LinkedIn as a viable-as-a-test direct-response customer generation platform.

I wanted to share the editing process of this book—and a solid example of me risking being dead wrong if I had not continued to believe that testing is learning and that things change in digital every single month—and this is proof that (a) you need to understand that opportunities and ad channel performance can change for the better or the worse over the course of one month, and (b) you need to keep your mind open, test, test, and test again and be ready to seize a good ROI opportunity while it lasts.

Who knows how much better or worse the advertising opportunities on social media platforms like LinkedIn will be when you read this at the end of 2019, and into 2020 and beyond?

But regardless of what social media channel or non-search digital channel we are talking about, below I will list some points you must put a priority on, and ignore what you think you know about what will and what will not work.

It is irrelevant *where* you find a person to advertise to vs. *who* that person is. The right ad served to the right person at the right price point with the right creative is the important equation to solve for in digital advertising, not where that person saw the ad.

I cannot stress enough that it simply does not matter where a person sees an ad. It does matter that you know things about them that make them an ideal customer. Are they the CTO you've been targeting? The rich person in the right neighborhood where you have a branch? Long gone are the days where the location of the advertisement—what was called "the placement" in the stone age of advertising and ruled the pricing of ads—is key. It's not entirely worthless to know where a person sees an ad, but it's so far down the line in terms of importance and actionable, essential data on an impression that it is nearly absent from best practice must-have pieces of data when optimizing campaigns.

Do you want your product or company's ad on a porn site? Probably not, unless you're in the adult entertainment space. But the value of putting your ad on the homepage of the local paper is as absurd as thinking that LinkedIn is for business, and Facebook or Instagram are not.

You're targeting humans more than you are targeting ad locations.

If we can target C-Level and VP-level decision makers who work at the correct companies (your target accounts), with additional filters of Household Income ("HHI") or Net Worth and dozens of other psychographic cues into these decision makers, then we as efficient digital marketers don't mind *where* they are seeing the advertisement and, thus, it offers no reason to pay a premium for location.

The days of the ad placement (website or page the ad is placed on) being important have nearly vanished. The ROI and CPL and CPA data is going to be different and each should be judged on a different basis.

Here are the facts: I've never yet seen one direct response campaign where LinkedIn beat Facebook in cost per customer acquisition. That might change in 2020 and beyond, but it hasn't happened yet in my extensive experience. So keep both the track record in mind and don't be fooled by thinking that placement (LinkedIn is for business, etc.) is the guiding light to smart media buying. But I'm also saying that while LinkedIn has not beat Facebook prior to 2020 from an ROI standpoint in terms of good leads and customers and good cost per acquisitions for B2B and High Value B2C, it doesn't mean that LinkedIn can't fix their challenges and do better in the future, therefore being worthy of your testing and budget going forward.

Bottom line: A person is not more valuable when they click on an ad on LinkedIn instead of CNN.com or Facebook. What matters is your volume of net new leads and customers and your cost to acquire each. And you've got to always be testing to make sure you don't ignore a formerly less successful ad channel that's finally getting it right from an ROI standpoint.

So if placement—the web page and location of an advertising impression—isn't the most important thing, what is?

THE MOST IMPORTANT THINGS ARE:

- Quality of the creative and ad being deployed (rich media or otherwise)
- Ability to target to the following levels and to combine these into a multi-layered profile:
  - Job title
  - Company
  - Household income, net worth, etc.
  - Education level/degree/program

- ° Prior life or work experience
- ° What they love
- ° What they need
- ° What happened in their lives to make them want or need your product
- ° Other key psychographic markers of a person

Be wary of any ad channel (e.g.: some newer paid ad models of struggling social media channels like Twitter, or display ad networks that promise to have a magic box of targeting that you can tap into) that has the following characteristics:

- ° The actual creative, meaning the images, videos, and text that it can deploy is not as good as what you can use on Facebook (again, Facebook is the gold standard for putting rich and powerful content in front of you)
- ° Only offers static images, instead of a robust video format, which is the new gold standard for B2B digital advertising.
- ° Does not offer multiple, dynamic products or ads within the same ad unit (like Facebook's amazing Collection ad portfolio or Carousel Ads, let alone the Canvas Ads).
- ° Beware if the ad channel offers ad formats where the creative is antiquated at best (hello, Twitter) and this fails to drive action and robustly convey a value proposition of a complex B2B or High Value B2C product.
- ° Only offers advertising on a CPM basis, which severely restricts your traffic and audience. Many ROI-suspect ad channels price only on a CPM basis. Facebook and other Tier 1 display ad networks do not have the severe scalability issue because they use a CPC basis (which, out of the gate, is safer when testing new campaigns vs. CPM). Make sure your channel isn't cutting off your audience or scalability by asking to test or run initially on a CPC basis.

○   The targeting is less robust than Facebook by an order of magnitude. The key is layering in many demographic and psychographic filters on top of one another. If you can only select from a limited list of targeting options. Some ad networks offer "Automotive" or "Banking" or some other ridiculously vague targeting pool w/o you having insight and control into each filter being applied.

Simply, LinkedIn may start to rival Facebook and Paid Search in terms of scale and ROI, and I have never been happier. The only thing a digital advertiser wants is options where they can spend money effectively. The more options the better, and it's possible that 2020 might be the year where we go from two main ad platforms (Google and Facebook/Instagram) to three.

That is not to say that Facebook works as well as SEM for all clients. Or that Facebook always succeeds for B2B. Or there aren't other levers that can work when you want a more limited scale for your business (e.g.: quarterly email drops are cheap but not scalable and hard to do with a good ROI every day; niche conferences; hosting a thought leadership summit, etc.). But Facebook does often compete and sometimes beats the ROI of search, certainly for products that are brand new, where few people are Googling the solution or product, or where it takes a video to explain the value. Moreover and at minimum, Facebook has become a must-have channel with a large percentage of a client's budget in many High Value B2C and B2B customer generation playbooks.

But that's the point of knowing which ad channels have a good track record of offering scale, good ROI, and being worth your time and teams who would become experts to protect and accelerate your business for years to come. And Facebook, of all the social media channels, is that essential piece in most digital portfolios.

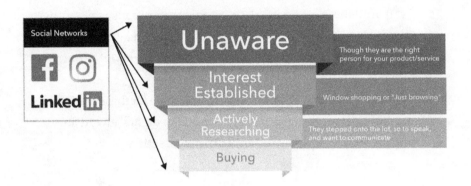

WHERE PAID SOCIAL MEDIA DOMINATES:
Brand Impact + Lead Generation

EVERY OTHER SOCIAL NETWORK

Pinterest, Snap, Twitter, Pandora, Spotify . . . and on and on. There is so much promise. But I'll make this short and sweet: as of 2020, they are not good for ROI+ customer generation. Period. I wish they were, but they simply are not.

Are they good for brand exposure or keeping in touch with current clients and enthusiasts of your product? Sure. But a waste of time if you're looking for a consistent, reliable stream of net new customers at good acquisition costs.

If you're reading this book and you care about low hanging fruit, quick ROI wins, and a scalable and proven media strategy that uses more advanced techniques in established digital channels to grow your business, these platforms are not what you are looking for. Not yet, at least. And per my notes above regarding the metamorphosis of LinkedIn, any of these platforms may yet get their direct response marketing act together and chance the landscape! But as of the writing (and re-writing) of this book, each of the social networks listed above is even more in its infancy than LinkedIn, for delivering an ROI to your marketing campaigns. So if you're looking to test beyond Google, Bing, Yahoo (again, this will shortly vanish altogether), Facebook/Instagram, and baseline banner ads and more advanced DSP-driven display, start with small spends on LinkedIn and wait until these others get their act together. Because these other social channels are, again, as of today, still for brand advertisers who care more about retweets and shares than they do about profitable customer generation.

But ask me again in 2024. Things might change for these platforms, a fact which is both the curse and the upside to digital advertising.

Maybe they can pull off a LinkedIn resurrection.

(3) A DIGITAL ADVERTISING GLOSSARY: THE CREATIVE

Lest we forget, marketing and advertising were for hundreds of years (TBD—but Gutenberg and John Calvin and his treatises nailed to the church door are good bookends) primarily about wordcraft and images. Pretty and/or compelling visuals and the poetry that made a product or service stick in your mind. Don Draper and the entire first wave of contemporary advertising were nothing more than catchy slogans and hand-drawn art made to pop off the page of magazines and newspapers. Nine out of ten doctors agree, after all.

And, while the appreciation and advanced deployment of the targeting and technology tools are *far* more important than crafting a single nifty slogan or ad campaign—because we live in a world where every niche of your dozens/hundreds of different consumers *can* be messaged as uniquely as you want!—words and images are still incredibly important.

The type of creative (words, images, etc.) needed to ensure efficiency in striving for better ROI isn't more important than it's ever been, but the *variety, volume* and *specificity* by-audience-type is. Let's start with two heavily used terms and their definitions, and also review the new mindset and checklist with what must be done in an effective marketing department in the 21st Century.

Creative = Anything a prospective customer sees or reads, such as visual or text-only advertisements, websites, or rich media content (visuals with more than a static image), which can help or hurt someone taking action.

UX/UI = User Experience, User Interface. This term often refers to the path a person is guided through on a website to use it, how those web pages look, where the navigation bar is which makes them scroll or not scroll or look around. These are what a viewer experiences when they are immersed in your web environment and the substance of the stuff they are consuming, learning, or made to do. UX/UI is also important to turn potential customers into customers, and often talked about when trying to make a marketing experience more effective for making an audience actually *do* something, but that's for a future discussion.

THE TWO TYPES OF ADS

Let's talk about the following things: what they are, why they are essential to deploy properly, and the best practices for each:

Advertisements used on the four digital channels above, which can be called different things (and some may disagree on the exactitude below), mostly fall into one of two categories:

1. Static Ad Units, Text Ad Units—Anything that is a single photo, design, image that doesn't move, or text-only.
2. Rich Media, Dynamic Ad Units
   - Anything that is not just a single image or design or photo
   - Animated images
   - Ads with video incorporated into them
   - Ad with multiple static images moving within it
   - Ad units with audio
   - Ad units with subtitles or text that flies around

Most professional designers, art directors, and digital project managers would disagree with the above oversimplification, and they'll have a point (e.g.: a dynamic ad unit can be a SEM ad that's just words but with a few of those words changing, based on the user's search query) . . . but it's more important to keep it simple for executives to be able to communicate with and lead their teams.

YOUR MESSAGING AND CREATIVE STRATEGY: WINNING THE CREATIVE BATTLE

Marketers, in particularly those trained in the old school where one message or ad campaign ruled the day, often miss the most essential strategy in effective 21st Century Marketing and, in fact, do the opposite!

The days of one message or one ad campaign slogan as the best strategy (I'm looking at your car dealers, banks, and other high-end retail) are dead.

Dead.

And if, in fact, you are clinging to the deceased world where Lucky Strikes were "toasted" and that's why they sold, then you're missing the most powerful element of what the internet has brought to bear: **Targeting**.

You can—and must—craft and test unique messages for every demographic and sub-demographic, every ad group in every SEM campaign, every ad set and psychographic targeting pool in social media . . . and for every product and service and territory you cover.

You can target each and nearly every single one of your current and prospective customers with words and images that they respond best to and don't have to believe that one size, one phrase, one image fits all.

Fifty years ago, we couldn't target people like we can now. Today, there is simply neither the logic nor the excuse to stick with limited messaging when we have the option to market test dozens if not hundreds of unique calls to action, images, videos, phrases and value proposition statements, seeing how *each* works for *each* granular ad group or campaign, then learning and building out more accordingly.

And in the vast majority of industries, the variety and intelligent aggression by which net new creative is churned out is massively underwhelming.

HIGH LEVEL STRATEGY CHECKLIST

While we will dive into this in the forthcoming Day 1 and Long-term Playbook chapters, there is a core premise that all progressive, effective marketers must embrace in the creative world. You need to ensure not only that your company looks unique and your value proposition is clear and compelling, but you need to do so differently than you did twenty-plus years ago. This newer ethos goes for the images and icons and stock photos and calls to action you use every word and visual that a current or prospective client sees. All of it.

My litmus test of a failed creative campaign is this: If you take your ad, video, campaign, etc.—any creative—and put one of your direct competitors' logos on it, and if it still makes sense, *you have failed.* That creative failed to answer the ultimate question: *Why are you different and better?*

How do you put the theme above—volume and data driven creative vs. old fashioned one-campaign-to-rule-them-all—into action?

- You need to start building out two to four different messaging themes you'll test over and over until there's a relevant result with every niche and segment listed above.
- You need to do a competitive analysis showing what others are doing and if there is (a) something you should copy/test, or (b) a hole in the messaging marketplace to test.

A piece of creative should help tell the story of why *your* company is right and everyone else is not It isn't necessarily important to tell your whole brand story in one banner ad, but the theme should be about differentiating you from them, and each ad and call to action should support this.

And to put into action and weaponize the theory above, this is your creative checklist for your marketing teams:

- Stop talking about which slogan is perfect, which image is perfect, which stock photo is perfect. **Stop thinking that you know best. Your customers will tell you what is working.** Simply, stop pontificating and start churning out new ads and copy *to test*.
- Make a ton of different ads and ad copy and image types, etc., and test multiple versions across every digital ad platform. Variety is key. Do it quickly and don't waste time after you get a statistically relevant answer.
- See what is working, by customer type, by product or service line, by ad platform, by geographic region, etc.
- Look at what the data (your customers' *actions*) tells you works.
- Learn from that and build out more.

(4) A DIGITAL ADVERTISING GLOSSARY: THE WEBSITES

Let's cut right to it. To a direct response, profit-focused marketing professional, there are only two kind of websites:

1. Main marketing websites
2. Landing pages

And you need both, in equal measures of investment and focus.

The bottom line is that if your company is not actively and aggressively deploying and optimizing landing pages by product, by division, by geo/rooftop, by customer type, by service line, you're losing to your competitors who are doing just that. Full stop.

In the olden days (let's call them the 2000s), companies used a precursor type of web environment for sometimes similar business outcomes that were called "microsites," which went extinct perhaps seven or more years ago. That happened because SEO and content strategies changed, and because the now-dominant mobile phones became powerful and popular as a way we consume content.

In prehistoric times (let's call them the 1990s), phones couldn't access the internet, and websites looked like pages torn from a small market newspaper's sports page.

We don't need to talk about your main marketing website or microsites.

We need to make sure that every company and executive reading this understands what landing pages are, and accepts that one cannot run an efficient High Value B2C or B2B customer generation marketing campaign without them.

The quick and dirty litmus test that everyone reading this must understand is that unless your company (a) has a website that was designed and built in the past 18 months to reflect true best-practice UX/UI, *and* (b) has the rare main website that only focuses on downloading an app or SaaS trial software and therefore is only worried about converting traffic to sales/downloads, then you cannot drive paid traffic of any kind (banner ads, search engine or social media ads, email campaigns, etc.) to your main marketing website (a homepage or a product page. It doesn't matter).

Simply: If you're not using landing pages, and your company does not meet the two requirements above, you are killing your ability to optimize a digital marketing campaign and you're lowering your ROI. Moreover, the best digital advertisers in the world cannot drive good results if they are driving traffic to a bad web environment.

That is neither subjective nor up for debate. And if you are the rare company and marketing executive who *is* deploying an intelligent army of landing pages, you'd be shocked at the percentage of CEOs and senior marketing executives who still treat this topic as either not necessary to be successful or not a priority.

But we will talk about landing pages more in depth as they are most certainly part of the Core Four.

(5) A DIGITAL ADVERTISING GLOSSARY: ESSENTIAL DATA, REPORTING, AND ANALYTICS CONCEPTS

Let's cut to the heart of what every company *must* be doing in 2020 and beyond, from a marketing reporting standpoint:

1. The most important thing in your marketing world, from a management and accountability standpoint, is reporting at minimum to the Cost Per Sale ("CPS") level.

2. You must be able, at minimum, to get this data point for each product or service line, and you must get this at minimum by advertising channel. Channels, as a reminder, are the four categories of digital experiences where humans are exposed to advertising, such as search engines, social networks, email campaigns, and banner ads. A platform, on the other hand, is a specific company within each of those channels. Google is a *platform* within the search engine *channel*.

3. If your marketing team or agency tells you they cannot report to this level of modest granularity, they are either (a) lying to you, (b) lying to themselves, (c) not trying hard enough using basic tools such as pivot tables in Excel.

The majority of C-level executives who run companies that do not have this essential KPI reporting down to—and hopefully beyond—the cost per sale level have been told that the technology is not there. That the "data is too fragmented" or stored in too many different places. That it's too difficult to track a person after a certain point.

90-95 percent of the time, **none of this is true.**

From billion-dollar companies founded two generations ago running a pre-SQL database to store customer info to 1-year-old SaaS startups looking to onboard SalesForce, it's not impossible.

Near-real time reporting? Switching between Cohort vs. Non-cohort views of your marketing and customer generation activity? That's much harder (oh, and we are going to cover Cohort vs. Non-cohort in a few pages, don't worry). But nearly any company, using some hard work and pivot tables or some basic reporting/database integrations, can give you the CPS on a monthly basis by channel, by product or service line.

But let's work on buzzword definitions and a checklist of things you'll need to understand before we dive into this world in future chapters. Keep in mind the following things:

1. It is essential to start with—and do well—the most simple, essential KPIs and the reporting around those data points before trying to create and absorb any other pieces of information or task your teams with any other spreadsheets. Trust me, most companies can't do the basics, but they try and get too fancy with too many reports and fail at everything. Keep it simple. Focus on a few KPIs.

2. Reporting is different than analytics. Reporting shows performance. Analytics takes a few different performance angles and trends and tells a story. You need performance reporting first.

So, how to get started with the essential and simple-to-focus-on and sometimes hard-to-create reports and KPIs? And what are the most important concepts when discussion these data points?

Cost Per Sale/Acquisition Reporting = Quite simply, the most important math concept in 21st Century Marketing. If your business is not following a customer from the time they click on an ad, through their journey on your website or landing page, into your sales funnel, and to the time they buy something, you are not doing marketing correctly.

The biggest mistake you can make is believing that you can't get this data and level of reporting with your current database or reporting tools.

If your marketing team or marketing agency tells you they simply cannot do this, I'm telling you that 90 percent of the time they are flat-out wrong.

I've seen hundreds of junkyard-level reporting and data storage environments, from businesses using tech twenty-five years old to companies whose websites can't be seen on a cell phone. And 100 percent of the time, I can at least figure out a way on a *manual reporting basis* to give a CEO the cost per sale by advertising channel, or at least a plan to get there in the next 60 days with minimum investment.

Now the solutions might not be down to the ad and campaign level (e.g.: the red banner ad has a 23 percent higher cost per sale in Facebook than the blue banner ads for boys 35-45 living in Boise named Sue), but you *can* absolutely and fairly cheaply and quickly (a) build a reporting solution to what their overall quarterly cost per sale is, and (b) set up some basic direct response tracking via unique phone numbers or digital ads and campaigns that pass in query string data into some data warehouse where you can match a click with a lead with a new customer.

DO NOT BE TOLD THAT YOU CANNOT DO THIS IN MARKETING FOR YOUR COMPANY. It's that simple.

BI Tool = Stands for "business intelligence" and it's often used as a catchall phrase to mean having at your fingertips (meaning an app on your phone or easily accessible web portal) the money you spend in marketing and the other activities (things that aren't tied to dollars but tied to work, such as PR articles or blog posts) being tied in *directly* to business outcomes you actually care about, like leads, sales, new customers, return customers, etc. The real versions of these tools can cut and slice your marketing and sales worlds by performance in any way you can dream of, on the fly. So, if you're looking at a report of all new leads and sales of one location or one product line for April 1through April 30, you should be able to use the tool to immediately see the by-ad-channel performance broken down by ad or day or week. There are a few parts to a BI Tool, but the thing you'll use visually to interface with has three big players—Tableau, Microsoft Power BI, and QlikSense (formerly QlikView). They sit on top of different kinds of databases or a data warehouse, and they typically need you to have a few people either in-house or on a consultancy basis to make sure these are running smoothly, which primarily means they make sure the data is *correct* and that data that gets put into these database/data warehouse repositories is reconciled and live (meaning that there are no broken connectors so you're not just missing whole chunks of data).

Cohort vs. Non-Cohort Data: If there is one thing you must understand as a marketer in the 21st Century regarding reporting, this is it. I have had hundreds of conversations for twenty years with CMOs and VPs—real, highly paid marketers—who cannot accurately explain the difference between these two things, and it completely destroys their ability to make good decisions because they simply cannot understand reporting, primarily between sales and marketing. The best metaphor I can use to explain the dissonance when people get these confused is that one is a musician playing Pachelbel's Canon in C Major and another musician is playing in D Major. The notes are slightly different, which is fine, but unless you read the key signature for each (meaning you know what notes get played via the little black keys on a piano), the C Major music would sound/look like nonsense to the D Major musician. Both are right, but appropriate for different types of ears.

- **Cohort** reporting is the natural, commonsense way that the **marketing world** works and communicates what is happening with your money and the performance of said money. Simply put, you spend money to get clicks and actions—leads submitted or calls made, or sales if you're in an eCommerce world—and you follow those exact people for a few weeks or months and *then* report on what they did, what they bought, and if they came back and bought more stuff, or if those leads became sales (in non-eCommerce worlds where sales cycles are longer than 24 hours). This is the only way you can mathematically, correctly tell a CMO or CEO how well the money was spent. You cannot get full cohort reporting immediately. It takes time for those humans you advertised to—and drove to your website to *do* something to, well, *do* something else, then *do* a few other things—to make their way down your sales funnel.

A good example of a cohort report is the essential Cost Per Sale analysis where, for example, you look at all the money that was spent in September, you measure all the leads that came in from those exact dollars, then follow those leads into October or November and beyond to see if they turned into sales. You then, ideally by ad channel and product/service line, divide the number of dollars spent in September by the number of sales that came from the leads that were created.

This, mathematically, tells you exactly how well your marketing team did with the most important KPI that speaks to return on marketing investment for September.

- **Non-Cohort** reporting is much more simple. It completely ignores following particular leads or customers for the days and months down their journey through your sales funnel. Non-cohort reporting is a sales-driven view of the world that only cares about stuff that happened in a specific time period.

This is what sales teams care about: How many sales did you get this month? How many leads were generated this week? We care because we have salespeople that need to work them and we need to staff appropriately.

Non-cohort reporting is used for sales and operations to see what type of sales activity is happening typically in the time period when the question is being asked.

The massive problem, however, is that you cannot use non-cohort reporting to report on how marketing is doing. It provides flat-out bad data and you cannot trust it.

Let me give you an example that, while extreme, can show you the potential for error when you try and use simple non-cohort reporting for *any* insight into how marketing is performing.

1. You have the same marketing budget the whole year, then pull back in December (it's the holidays, and your sales team is taking a ton of days off and you run a non-CPG business that doesn't make sense to compete with all the expensive impression inventory that's being gobbled up by everyone selling toys or electronics). Your budget goes from super steady to a low point in December.

2. You run a simple non-cohort report.

3. You run a report that is more complicated to track, but more granular in seeing what is happening with your money.

4. The difference in your Cost Per Lead and Cost Per Sale in December is massively different as are your results the few months to follow.

5. This difference between the cohort and non-cohort view of your marketing world will happen 100 percent of the time whenever your budgets change month to month or quarter to quarter. If the changes are not that large, and if they don't change much by channel, this isn't that big a deal. But for every dollar in delta month to month in spend, you're risking massive bad data when you run a non-cohort report and make marketing decisions based off that information.

Average Lead-to-Sale Maturation Time = 1 Month	August	September	October	November	December	January	February
media spend	$0	$200,000	$200,000	$200,000	$50,000	$300,000	$50,000
leads	—	1,000	1,000	1,000	250	1,500	250
cohort sales		100	100	100	25	150	25
non-cohort sales			100	100	100	25	150
cost per cohort sale		$2,000	$2,000	$2,000	$2,000	$2,000	$2,000
cost per non-cohort sale			$2,000	$2,000	$500	$12,000	$333

REPORTING vs. ANALYTICS

Before we dive into how to take your baseline reporting to the next level, beyond making sure the key tactics and technology pieces that need to be present in your marketing and sales view of the data (which will be at the very end of this book in Chapter 4, Section 8), it is essential to make sure when you *do* take the first steps, they are the right ones. We need to make sure you're not wasting time which, as you'll see below, is a lot more tempting and common than you think as you grow into a mature world of advanced campaign measurement and deep analytics.

DATA IS THE MOST DANGEROUS WORD IN MARKETING

What is the most important thing to keep in mind after the block-and-tackling Core Four elements (Chapter 3) are stood up in your company in terms of data? As digital marketers and executives, we need to only focus on the data, reports, and analytics that matter rather than the vanity metrics and expensive SaaS platforms that make executives feel good but contribute very little in the way of actionable information.

Specifically, if a piece of technology or a cadre of data fails to do at least one of the following things in marketing, it is a waste of time and money:

1. Help your company better target your ideal client
2. Help reach and acquire your target customer for less money
3. Help optimize your cross-channel marketing mix for better overall ROI

You may be wondering "why?" Who could possibly hate a shiny new piece of tech or more data? Let me explain.

WHY THE WORD DATA IS DANGEROUS

Data is dangerous because it is the ultimate lethal buzzword. First, it commands near-ubiquity status as a pure and good thing. Data is considered the universal must-have. Have you ever heard any business professional say, "We need less data" or "We don't need data for this project"? No. Never. It is the professional version of the word love or happiness. Does anyone hate love or want less happiness? Of course not. When something is universally demanded, it gets on every must-have list on every digital marketing project in the world.

Second, the word data has no real, granular meaning because it is so overused and misused that it essentially becomes a worthless phrase unless you're not shooting for tangible goals tied to data outcomes. Simply, the word "data" is often void of an actual outcome in our business lives because it has become so widely used that you could basically replace it with the word "numbers" and mean the same thing.

When you combine a must-have marketing buzzword with a phrase that is now absent of a specific outcome, it means you're going to be doing a bunch of "stuff" that is not tied to a larger strategy. And that's a prime scenario for wasting time and money on a thing that isn't helping you move the needle in your business, from a marketing standpoint.

REAL WORLD EXAMPLES

The most common example of how the word "data" is dangerous can be seen within your company's core marketing and sales reporting in terms of ad campaign performance. At every company I've worked for and in (including my own), when it comes to the idea of data in sales and marketing, this usually means you're going to churn out a bunch of reports and Excel spreadsheets that do not actually help you do anything better from, you guessed it, a sales and marketing standpoint. The reports will not tell you how to do something faster or with a better outcome.

Why not?

First, most business people use the word "analytics" when they really mean "reporting" (often because they want to sound fancy), and they're actually misusing the term in terms of their goals and business outcomes. To review, a report conveys the performance of a campaign whereas analytics tells a story. I would contend that the first thing—performance—is the greatest example of a simple, baseline metric essential for any marketing or sales goal but is very often not present, or uses the wrong numbers with bad data. In fact, it is the must-have element in running sales and marketing: How did a campaign or effort perform? So, people ignore a good, baseline performance report and focus on a fancier and less important thing which is, using the correct term, analytics.

Second, when business people say they need analytics, they actively shop for and buy advanced analytics software when they don't even have good baseline reporting to begin with. Baseline reporting is cheaper, easier to deploy and way more important to have than advanced analytics. So, not only do people not know what they really need (a simple report that shows, in most cases, the cost per acquisition for marketing campaigns by line item), but they ignore the basics and try and get fancy with things referred to as analytics. Unfortunately, they do not get any meaningful benefit with the more advanced solution, either. Two good examples of fancy SaaS solutions that are much less valuable than having baseline performance reports but leapfrog in importance (and are orders of magnitude more expensive than creating baseline reports) are lead scoring and BI tool implementations. I would argue that both of those things are worthless compared to baseline performance reports of an active campaign, and it takes many months or years it takes to deploy these solutions that cost five or six figures.

It's akin to buying a car without an engine and instead worrying about the paint color, or spending a lot of extra time and money on a stereo upgrade . . . and where the engine costs a fraction of the price. I'm not saying a nice new paint job or a great sound system is bad, but without an engine, a car is as worthless as a marketing or sales campaign is without baseline reporting that shows total cost per acquisition by campaign/by channel.

Another great example would be attribution models, which I'd define broadly as the attempt to use analytics to more correctly determine what ad channel should be given credit for a sale or, rather, how much more or less credit should be given versus relying on only "last click" understandings.

Many companies fail to focus on a simple, perhaps manual process of getting better insights into what is happening *before* the last click—and understanding how much those things cost and how valuable those actions were in the overall marketing funnel. I have seen countless examples of a team that ignores nailing down these baseline elements and instead, gets sold on a fancier version of an attribution model that requires huge amounts of money spent up-funnel and maybe has a super amazing interface built by a very expensive SaaS company.

The problem is that if that model isn't a zero-sum game (meaning that you're inflating the performance of the whole company's marketing to try and make sense of the sales funnel . . . which is bad), it is a great example of data that is a waste of your time. Or if you can't agree as a company on an attribution model that you will adopt when you did it manually—and in-house—before you ran out and bought an expensive platform, then you've made a huge mistake. Are these fancier versions fun to look at? Sure. Do they make executives feel good that they are doing fancy things by tracking their customers well before the last click to purchase? Absolutely. But it's not actually useful to help a digital media buyer spend money better or help a company better deploy their ad budget. Useful would be either a simple, manual attribution analysis *or* ignoring attribution altogether and just focusing on doing better with last-click media buying.

Does this mean I'm against full-stack, best-in-class attribution models? No! Heck, my company is in this world to build things like that! But to use data to actually help your company, you may just need better reporting. Not even better analytics, but rather good old-fashioned reporting. What most companies really need is more accurate data and reporting that focuses on either better targeting your customers or better optimizing your digital marketing campaigns.

Good reporting should always include the following three elements:

1. Lead with the main Key Performance Indicator (KPI). Report on the single most important metric first. That will ensure that the most essential detail isn't missed when measuring results (there is frequently the urge to over-report and show too much information). An important marketing KPI to measure against is the Cost Per Acquisition, which calculates how much it costs to acquire a new customer.

2. In terms of marketing reporting, if you are not pulling in sales and customer data from your CRM (even it's manual) and marrying it up to your front-end budgets to see real results, you're likely not looking at what is truly a KPI. Instead, it is often a vanity metric that isn't used to make your marketing operations better.

3. Automate the reporting as much as possible so that after you have built a simple report starting with your KPIs, you don't have to waste time compiling the same pieces of information together weekly. It can be as complex as hiring a firm that specializes in creating, building, launching and training your team on an advanced BI tool like Tableau or QlikSense or Power BI or it can be a simple automation of marrying Excel spreadsheets together. You need to get smarter with the time you spend on combining disparate data sources together.

4. That's it. Sometimes it's less data, not more. If you want to optimize your digital marketing campaigns, ignore the hailstorm of white noise in data and marketing and *cover the basics first.*

So while we are not going to review the more advanced types of analytics until the very end of this book, and it's essential per what we just talked about to keep it simple when you first dive into ensuring your reporting and data is done right, it is important to note that your customer's journey into your sales funnel happens way before the day they clicked on an ad. Here are two visualizations showing what most companies see as the sales funnel, and what the sales funnel in the 21st Century really looks like.

In a *REAL* Marketing Funnel

TARGET

CUSTOMER

Browsing Time ▶ Shopping Time $$$ Lead or Sale

In the real world, people see your advertisements across search engines, social networks, banner ads and email campaigns...not to mention offline behavior. And sometimes the ad isn't the right ad or the right time for them to click to learn more...and it's important to understand that seeing an ad has value, but seeing an ad + going to your website/landing page is more valuable

What does this all mean?

It means that your customers are often "born" well before Day 0. In the chart below, this is a fairly accurate view into where a person starts to know about your company before they officially get into your outbound sales funnel efforts:

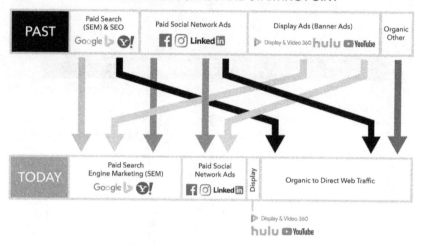

Again, while we'll talk at the very end of Chapter 4 (Section 8) about more advanced reporting via BI tools that effectively compute zero-sum attribution models, it is important even at the beginning of your marketing and sales funnel data comprehension journey to see what's really going on.

(6) A DIGITAL ADVERTISING GLOSSARY: PAY PER LEAD ("PPL") AFFILIATES VS. PROPRIETARY ADVERTISING

I considered not including a section on defining and explaining at a high level what pay per lead ("PPL") affiliate vendors do, when they are essential, and who needs to dive in and become an expert for the good of their role in their industry. There just aren't that many marketers, as an overall percentage, that should or can care, because the PPL industry doesn't exist across every vertical or niche in business, rather only a dozen or so at large scale. But to *not* talk about the niche—nearly always either ROI-and-brand-dangerous or massively beneficial purely depending on your personal knowledge of the space, and rarely well understood by those on the outside the PPL "inner circle" of lead creators in a playbook about marketing—is like not talking about YoYo Ma, John Coltrane, or They Might Be Giants when talking about 20th Century music. While, as an overall percentage of music listeners, each of these artists are the favorite musician of very few people, those who *are* fans are massive fans. Those who thrive on that style of music—baroque cello, blues, and happy scrappy funny pop, respectively—simply cannot survive without one of these groups being in the conversation.

The same is true for the PPL affiliate industry and understanding 21st Century Marketing. For a small group of high-margin, high demand-side industries (for-profit higher education, home mortgage, and car insurance sectors and to a lesser extent more wild-west industries such as diet pills and more high margin, illiquid markets like home improvement), PPL vendors are *the* lifeblood. Companies like Geico, Quicken, University of Phoenix and hundreds of massive corporations literally would not exist as we know them today without the PPL Affiliate market.

So if you're in one of these industries, I'm preaching to a tired choir as you've ridden the wave of your industry's peaks and valleys by buying more or less PPL as the main lever of your net new customer acquisition. You've fought the fight of lower quality, lower conversion rates for what feels like a billion years, had the same recycled conversations about compliance and lack of brand control, and—most importantly—still spend a massive amount of money because the PPL Affiliate channel has often driven the most new customers for the best cost per acquisition at high volume.

Call it a necessary evil or call it a channel to master for the good of your company. But you better call it the backbone of your growth and marketing agility, like it or not.

For everyone else: Pay attention. Understand that while there might not be a PPL market and PPL affiliates active in your industry, you should verify that. If they exist, they might be worth testing, but that is a dangerous market for inexperienced novice marketers to dip their toes into. Like the sucker at a poker table, if you can't tell the difference between the legitimate players and the shady ones, or where Vendor A and Vendor B are getting their leads, you *are* the sucker.

But here is a high level of the PPL Affiliate market from someone who has owned and operated a multi-million dollar pay per lead generation company in a prior life (I launched a higher education focused PPL company in 2010 and sold it in 2017 and worked in the sector on the client side for three and a half years prior).

WHAT IS A PPL AFFILIATE COMPANY OR VENDOR?

A pay per lead (again, it's nearly always referred to as just "PPL") affiliate is a company whose mission in life is to collect consumer information and sell that data to the highest bidder, or multiple bidders. They never actually run a business in the space. Lead sellers don't actually run schools, or insurance companies, or mortgage empires or sell diet pills. They create an environment—maybe a website or portal, maybe run another business that provides content or a service for consumers—that has access to your personal contact information. These companies get your permission because you use their primary service for free (social networks, industry blogs, product review websites, etc.), and then sell your information to companies that then try and sell you stuff.

Or you are signing up for a job board—which is often free for you to use—but you have given that portal access to your name, address, phone number, etc., etc. which is how that company makes money to provide you with that free service.

Though they are the pariahs of the sales and marketing world, it's pure hypocrisy for consumers to hate their existence. Don't like the idea of companies using your information to make money to provide you with a "free" service? Then go live in a world where you need to pay to use the following websites every month:

- Facebook
- Instagram
- LinkedIn
- U.S. News & World Report
- Monster.com
- Every other job site in the world
- Every web site that gives you free content that they create
- Any free credit report, free product or service or industry review website, etc.

Every company above is either a direct lead generator (i.e., they directly sell your data to their clients) or they weaponize your data and web behaviors and info you gave them. They use it to allow smart advertisers to show you ads for stuff you actually might care about (instead of stuff you would never buy, which is the strategy of every social network).

But the difference between PPL vendors and everyone else providing content or an experience (Facebook, for example) is that the PPL vendor sells your data as-is, or they directly weaponize your data (like running everyone in their database through a call center) to *make* a lead to sell. Facebook doesn't sell your data. I use Facebook as an advertiser on their platform to show you ads of things you actually might care about, and my efforts have enough people clicking where I want them to click, going to the website and landing page where I want them to go to, and each one becomes a lead or a customer because I've done my job.

PPL vendors straight up sell data as leads, or they take data, run it through a user experience or call center, and make a lead to sell.

WHY DO THEY EXIST?

They typically exist in hyperbolic markets where the supply and demand curves are, for a lack of a more refined academic adjective, completely messed up, and where aggregate demand far outstrips supply, and the profit margins for each new customer are high. Then you have companies that see that there is a business to be made as a middleman, that is, a connector between the (limited) supply and the (near infinite) demand.

With names like CrazyCheapInsurance.com or QuoteCompare or ClassesUSA or RefinanceCalculator or Franchise Gator (some of those are fake, some are real . . . but that's part of the lesson here), these websites do not run schools or insurance companies or are the franchise company itself. Instead, they offer a type of a service, the quality of which is debatable and for another book . . . and in exchange for this free data, they sell your info.

Again, the best examples are the for-profit education, the mortgage, and personal insurance (auto) verticals. Other examples absolutely exist in other industries—maybe yours—but are more difficult to navigate, though again, essential to explore as they can be incredibly profitable . . . with the right management.

It is important to mention that some PPL vendors actually make leads without monetizing their own database and, like your company, advertise on search engines and social networks. But there are two massive differences:

1. They can use ads and calls to action you'd never be able to use (often toe-on-the-line of being aligned with your brand and the overall degree of aggression).

2. They can monetize general traffic you'd never be able to drive to your website and landing page and convert (e.g.: the keyword "online school" cannot be responsibly bid on by any school where that school has a good ROI on that keyword, but a PPL can).

WHAT ARE THEY GOOD FOR?

They can provide your business and your competitors with massive new leads at a low price and in product or service lines or in geographic areas where you are having a hard time getting lead flow for, but for which they already have an existing pipeline.

They can often afford to pull in this volume because, in your industry, they sell *everything* . . . and they therefore can cast a net much wider than you can as a marketer selling just one company.

WHAT ARE THE TYPICAL WAYS PPL COMPANIES MAKE LEADS?

Of every lead sold, over 80 percent comes through some kind of call center. Anyone who tells you differently is lying. No one gets the majority of their profit in selling leads "from SEO." If someone representing a lead gen company tells you this, throw them out of your office.

If your PPL agency tells you that most of the vendors they're getting your leads from are "mostly SEO," fire them and then throw them out of your office.

Sure, some actually deploy money on search engines and social networks and drive people to their portals, or they use email campaigns or buy exit traffic from other sites or get aggressive via SMS text . . . but who cares?

Honestly, stop worrying about where leads come from. Worry about the ROI.

I've spent a decade alongside and inside many of the largest, most well-funded and well-staffed verticals where clients employ hundreds of lawyers and tens of millions of dollars on fancy pieces of tech that sniff out naughty lead seller tactics.

But if you're already heavily invested in the PPL market, you likely don't really care, just like the dozens of amazing and ethical CXOs who say one thing on compliance and marketing calls, but say another to the CFO and Wall Street when they talk about ROI and top line growth. You'll say you care about your brand or your litigation risk or your new customer experience, but the next day you want to break every egg to make that ROI omelet. I don't say this antagonistically. I say this to encourage you to be honest with the goals and the methods you use, thinking they are an acceptable risk for your business and marketing and sales funnel.

My advice: If you're going to buy from the PPL market, do it and understand that there does not exist a world with PPL that doesn't have some risk.

Or, don't touch the PPL channel, but know that some of your competitors are taking that risk and besting you to make more money, grow faster, and being more dynamic with their growth.

You can't have it both ways, regardless of what some SaaS company has told you. You can't participate in the PPL marketplace and be 100 percent safe from a compliance and brand-integrity standpoint. That's just a fact but keep in mind, there are always risks running your own internal proprietary advertising efforts, albeit the risks are lower. And if I'm being a bit cagey and not naming names for the exact services I'm referring to, it's because there are only a few larger companies selling "marketing and data insight" or "customer journey insight" for big dollars, because I think that the ROI and the ultimate business outcome is questionable for most digital marketing scenarios versus their cost, but also because in some situations, these significant investments can pay for themselves.

WHY ARE THERE INCREASED RISKS COMPARED TO YOUR OWN PROPRIETARY DIGITAL ADVERTISING?

You'll be getting leads and customers exposed to high pressure, low information sales experiences before they came to your doorstep and there is nothing you can do to ensure that their journey was 100 percent OK with your brand. Sometimes, the only exposure these leads get to your brand is a 100x100 pixel logo on some makeshift microsite or sometimes, just a radio button with the name of your company. And sometimes there is more information about your exact company and product, and the affiliate company has a tremendous web experience, but it's never as robust or as brand-right as your own digital world, obviously.

But depending on the vertical, the harsh reality is that often doesn't matter. Like, at all, regardless what your compliance team is telling you. I have only seen a few instances out of hundreds and hundreds of companies engaging in the affiliate market suffer significant consequences for compliance breaches; the vast majority profited massively and never regretted it. And those that did suffer did so because of the greed and mismanagement of their marketing teams who did not pay attention to obvious warning signs of quality concerns and questionable, overly aggressive tactics.

WHAT IS THE SPECIFIC UPSIDE?

In the few industries where they operate, PPLs are where you'll find the lowest cost per customer acquisition, the largest volume of new customers, and with the least amount of marketers to manage it. Bottom line: For a few industries, PPL is the best, most scalable lead source with some of the lowest cost per acquisition performance.

SHOULD YOU DO IT?

You'll need to be the judge on whether you engage in the PPL market, but I would strongly urge you at least consult with, if not engage and hire, a mid-size or large agency with deep experience in both the affiliate market as a buyer and, ideally, experience with your affiliate vendors who deal with your specific industry. Such agencies can also help be arbiters regarding feasibility for your exact corporate situation, and use of expensive bells and whistles such as lead management technology or some of the prior-mentioned data insight SaaS services, and what the costs will be.

TIPS TO HIRE A PPL AGENCY

If you do hire an agency to run your digital marketing, including the PPL channel, I would strongly recommend that you under-pay them for their work in PPL compared to the other digital work. This doesn't mean don't pay them well—on behalf of my agency brethren, please pay good money for good work—but you must incentivize them to weight their focus on succeeding in your proprietary digital advertising.

Why would a guy who is the CEO of a digital agency recommend under-paying companies like mine for a certain type of work?

- Because the very lowest hanging fruit and lowest cost per acquisitions for leads are the baseline proprietary digital advertising methods. We will be covering them in Chapter 3. You should use these methods before anything else, including running PPL affiliates.
- Because you still need to have your brand in the digital marketplace, and PPL vendors flat out are not good at giving your brand exposure. That's not their value. You need to do that yourself.
- Because it's safer. As I said before, there are some not very good affiliates among the very good ones, so it's hard to find a great PPL agency. There is more risk to your brand than in-house proprietary digital advertising that treats your brand like it's the most important thing in the world. An affiliate's job is to connect people with a good offer among many companies.
- *And to directly answer the question of "Why incentivize your agency to focus on proprietary digital versus PPL?"*

  ○ Because it takes a tremendous amount of creative and technical work to get you leads and customers in proprietary digital advertising like search engines, social networks, and display ads,

  ○ Because to get more leads in PPL, you need to do little more than pick up the phone and call a few affiliate vendors.

  ○ Because if you pay an agency based on a percent of the media dollars, like most marketing contracts, and it takes 20 percent as much work to spend $100,000 in PPL versus real proprietary digital advertising on Google, Bing, Facebook, LinkedIn and banner ads, then the agency will tend to overspend in PPL rather than work to be exceptional in doing the real in-platform work in the actual digital advertising channels. Simply, it's harder to run what we will call proprietary (meaning you are advertising your company) digital advertising to drive new customers than it is to email a PPL vendor and buy leads.

° This is not saying PPL is a bad choice or you should only do digital advertising, but you need to understand that when you contractually position the carrot facing in one specific direction, don't be surprised when your agency chases that carrot. And you need to right-price an agency's fees based on how much real work something takes.

What I've just said is fairly incendiary, and I'm sure a lot of agencies will disagree. But I've done both PPL buying and proprietary digital advertising as an agency of record as a CEO, owner, and also have been the actual person in the trenches doing the actual jobs of media buying and lead buying. I've done that for about 20 years and have spent probably close to $100,000,000 in the process, and I'm right: PPLs are not really incentivized to be honest.

And besides, my agency offers PPL affiliate management as a service, so if I'm suggesting you slightly disincentivize an agency's work in this area, you should take my word for it.

CHAPTER 2

The Essential Marketing Strategy and Team Structure for Every Company

IT'S IMPORTANT THAT WE TALK ABOUT the general steps or activities in the new or return customer journey, which combines different ad channels and tactics into buckets of activity to answer the question: *Why should you do this?*. We are not yet going to dive into the granular tactics. First, we'll answer the *what* and the *why* and, most importantly, the essential setup.

At a high level, you need to know that the journey in B2B and High Value B2C net new customer generation is a path that follows this flow:

1. Drive consumer action
2. Convert actions into leads
3. Convert leads into customers
4. Optimize using data to spend a dollar better today than you did yesterday.

Stages of the High Value
B2C and B2B Sales Cycle

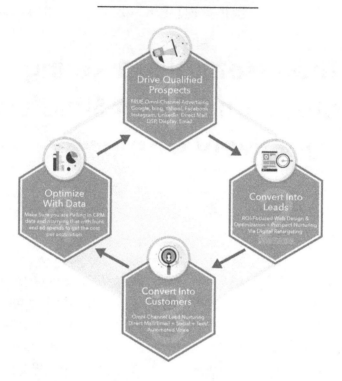

And while infographics are nice, we need to talk more about why we do this, beyond the fact that it's better, smarter, and respects ROI and the core desired outcome of marketing.

- We want to take media dollars and turn those into new B2C customers and qualified sales opportunities for B2B companies.
- We want to only focus on what we know makes money 90 percent of the time, activities that have proven to show a Return on Marketing Investment.

But beyond the steps, let's talk about the WHY.

It is essential that you know it is irrelevant that you (or your SVP or whoever) doesn't use Facebook. It does not matter that

you've never bought something after searching on Google. It's not germane that no one opens email, or that direct mail is old and therefore dumb. Or that you're in a legacy industry and this isn't for you. Or that you think that you have to impress the world with viral videos to make money.

So let's talk about *why*.

THE RELIGION OF DIGITAL AND DIRECT RESPONSE

I want to convert you to the data driven culture of companies who have embraced 21st Century Digital and Direct Marketing. It's not based on the false gods of your feelings or the anecdotal "I think" mindsets of your forefathers' marketing practices. It's a newer marketing belief system (circa October 2000 with the birth of Google AdWords) where every dollar is held accountable for a Return On Investment, and where 21st Century Digital works hand in hand with traditional sales practices to drive results.

In the majority of our conversations with CEOs, Presidents, and Chief Marketing Officers and VPs of Marketing regarding their confidence in the quantifiable, 100-percent attributable understanding of the exact customer generation outcomes of their marketing campaigns, there is a consistent answer: **They have little confidence, and almost none when it comes to the direct relationship to ROI from said customer generation efforts.**

Specifically, they have little insight into what current 2017 best practices should be in play and, nearly as often, no answer the most basic question: **What was our marketing ROI (MROI) or return**

on advertising spend (ROAS)?

These executives sometimes believe that their companies simply don't have the technology or data access required to use direct response customer generation that tracks ROI 100 percent back to the ad or campaign level.

The marketing world, they have been told and they have come to believe, is flat.

So they resign themselves to the most dangerous thought of the marketing Dark Ages (the days pre-internet) that CORRELATION = CAUSATION. **In other words, "we've always done it this way, and we're still in business. So it must be working!"**

But the world is *not* flat.

Marketing *absolutely* must have an ability to report and focus on ROI first; only then can less ROI-certain activities occur.

And no type of marketing gets a free pass.

Billboards and TV must be held as accountable as paid social network ads and search engine marketing. All show a combination or words/sounds and images, so why should the old school get a pass? PR must be held to the same standard as affiliate marketing or paid social media. Direct mail, conferences, events, print ads in industry journals . . . all of these strategies must do their share, and do their share where you can quantify the ROI by division and by line item. In a world where budgets are not infinite, you should only pick the ones where there is a provable ROI. **If you can't track it, why in the world would you invest heavily in it?**

But these definitive, trackable, quantifiable marketing channels *do* **exist in every industry.** This isn't 1985.

Living in the decision tree rooted in the world of anecdotal "evidence" is dangerous when your competition isn't doing the same. Resting on marketing tactics that were invented when your father or mother ran the company, or when an MBA who graduated in the Reagan administration wrote them, will kill your company, sooner or later.

Marketing fundamentals have changed, in addition to the tactics and tools. Run a marketing strategy that smacks of the 1980s and the marketplace will ensure you end up on the bottom. Everything top to bottom has changed because now you can spend money in customer generation and direct and digital marketing and measure every penny and have a good chance of success. There are so many tools available and most don't take advantage.

At the end of the day, I care about trackable and provable ROI.

Anyone who tells you they care about anything else doesn't share your goals.

Brand marketing? That's fine. Typically, that's the only thing that's being done because it's easier and a well-worn path, and there are fewer moments where you can point to exactly what failed.

Brand marketing is what you do when you're 100 percent positive that your customer generation marketing engine is working well.

So let's set some expectations and then talk about getting your customer generation marketing engine going.

THE ESSENTIAL STRATEGIC ELEMENTS IN 21ST CENTURY MARKETING

With great access to data comes great responsibility. Every marketing campaign will have the following list of features as consistent thematic drivers and goals, regardless of ad channel—these should be your baseline expectations for weekly, monthly, and quarterly check-ins with your marketing team or agency:

Simply, if you're not forcing/confirming the existence of these things at the strategic marketing and planning level, you're already lost.

1. ESSENTIAL EXPECTATIONS

In general, the goal for both short term and long-term best practice customer generation marketing is to build "need-to-have" vs. "nice-to-have" digital advertising campaigns across all digital and direct marketing channels that are likely to drive return on marketing investment ("ROMI") and, in addition, the necessary landing pages to drive new customers at effective cost per client acquisition figures. Moreover, there must be, at minimum, daily reports and, in an ideal long-term scenario, near real-time report across every channel (digital and direct) clearly showing mid-funnel KPIs as well as the ultimate Cost Per Customer Acquisition—the most important metric in the world of marketing.

If this is an outsourced relationship where there is an agency in lieu of a full stack internal marketing team, the agency must allow the client 100 percent transparency into reporting, media costs vs. agency costs, and read-only access to the actual advertising platforms. You would be terrified to know how many agencies still markup media or third-party fees. It's borderline criminal and in my opinion completely unjustifiable profit-taking with no added value.

From a planning standpoint, the goal is to create two things: the strategic media plan which would consist of applied tactics and associated costs with a primary focus on building the digital marketing infrastructure that will drive new qualified sales leads at an effective cost per acquisition for both a short term/Day 1/Phase 1; and a longer term marketing strategy and portfolio. These two are different.

2. ESSENTIAL KPIs

For digital advertising and customer generation related campaigns, the most frequently used main KPIs are Volume of Qualified Sales Leads and Cost Per Customer (or Cost Per Acquisition/CPA). Those are the two most important factors and most likely to be used in not only short-term optimization conversations by your teams actually doing the media buying, but also in terms of speaking to the general, overall efficacy and benefit of each ad channel and ad platform (e.g.: a channel example is Search Engines or Social Networks, an ad platform is Google or Facebook).

Ultimately, after six or more months of activity and allowing leads to convert into customers *vis a vis* best effort sales practices, the KPI will also be a profitability analysis because every customer is not the same; some keep buying and buying and staying with your product or service, and some only engage and purchase once.

But let's get more specific:

- The most important thing to you as the CEO or executive in charge of marketing is the Cost Per Acquisition or Cost Per Sale, that is, the total marketing cost that it costs your company to get one more customer or sale. We typically talk about that final KPI in the long term such as in quarterly or annual business reviews; and sometimes on monthly calls, if the sales cycles or volume of new sales in your ecosystem warrant that.
- On a daily basis, you can manage and hold teams accountable by speaking to Cost Per Lead or Cost Per _____ (insert good early customer touchpoint) KPIs that are typically called "mid-funnel" because that action is the step *before* the sale or *before* the final desired customer outcome for your company. Maybe that's Cost Per Appointment or Cost Per Qualified Lead, if you're running a B2B company where it's a big deal to be sitting down with a lead and knowing that they're real, and they're actually interested in your company. Unless you run an eCommerce platform where most customers *do* buy within five minutes of the click, then your daily management metric is different than the monthly, quarterly, or annual KPI of the Cost Per Acquisition or Cost Per Sale granddaddy, KPI.

Keep in mind that your teams will NOT optimize their daily work using CPA or CPS. Instead, they'll use early-funnel or mid-funnel metrics (cost per click, cost per lead) not because these are the most important to your business, but because:

- The "value" of each lead by channel is typically static in the mid-term. Google leads generally convert the same from Lead to Sale for the same product or service lines month after month unless there is a massive shift in how humans use Google, which doesn't happen too often.

- To manage digital ads correctly, you need to see changes on an hourly or daily basis and react accordingly. This means your teams need to rely on Cost Per Clicks or other actions and measurements *inside* the ad platform to do their work.

- Leads will be generated. Keep in mind that, again, some data points and variables *can* be ostensibly held static if you run a good digital marketing team. The conversion rate of a click to a lead on your landing page or website does change when you improve the website or landing page, but a media buyer in Google must assume that to run their daily Google optimizations correctly, they need to hold click-to-lead rates constant or improve.

- Though you don't really need to fully understand this, you *do* need to let your team manage on a daily basis by cost per clicks and cost per leads, and in the long term still hold them accountable for Cost Per Qualified Leads and Cost Per Sale/Acquisitions.

  As it has been said before, at an executive level and in the long term, the final and most important KPI is Cost Per Sale or Cost Per Acquisition (CPS or CPA).

  ° For non-digital advertising projects, the KPI is On Time/On Budget. The most common examples are creative tasks or back/front end web development.

°   For customer generation campaigns and digital advertising, the KPIs will be Cost Per Customer Acquisition and Cost Per Engagement (for existing clients *vis a vis* getting a higher utilization rate).

3. ESSENTIAL ROLES FOR YOUR TEAM

It is your responsibility to know at a high level what you need your employees to actually do in marketing. If you don't understand what needs to get done and the types of people who need to do, you are not on the best path to getting the results you want, and will be surprised when your strategy isn't driving results. Strategy needs execution. Work needs the right people to do it.

You're the boss, and the boss needs to be able to call b.s. and critique/curate the marketing battle plan.

As such, every marketing campaign in every phase will require the following support. If the following humans and responsibilities below aren't being deployed for every campaign, they will likely fail.

A.   Daily optimization of all campaigns on the level of Cost Per Click and, most importantly, Cost Per Lead, and Monthly/Quarterly optimization on lower funnel KPIs (such as Cost Per Sale and Cost Per New Customer Acquisition). We will, again, call these early-funnel or mid-funnel metrics.

- You need media buyers who understand the roles below as well as people who can acquire, combine, and report on the data necessary to show how your campaigns are running. Sometimes, you can find these skillsets in a single media buying team. Other times you'll need both an analytics team and a media buying team. Either way, you need people who get data and make actionable, ROI-communicative reports. And you need people who use this data and these reports every day to change their behaviors and bidding and management of the digital advertising channels.

- These early and mid-funnel metrics will require marrying at least two reports (where the money was spent, and the CRM report of the number of leads created or actions taken) to arrive at a Cost Per Lead basis at the campaign level to ensure ROI. (See chart below to understand where the term "campaign level" fits into the hierarchy of digital advertising.) The campaign level is one step below ad channel and is the minimum acceptable degree of reporting granularity you should accept. A quick note on how digital marketers talk about their family tree and parent/child relationship of their media world:

How Digital Marketers Talk About Their Media: Terms and Ad Channels/Platforms

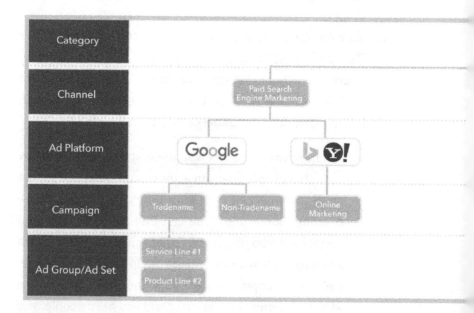

- The numerator in this case (Cost/Leads) must include both media costs as well as agency costs (Advertising Costs + Agency Fees). You can just use the media fees to talk about CPL, but at the end of the day at the executive level (maybe in monthly but definitely in quarterly and annual reports) you need to understand what is called the full marketing ROI.
- If you want to get fancy, you'll start to understand the fully baked cost to create a customer in your company on an annual basis in your P&L deep dive by looking beyond just to the cost to advertise plus the cost to hire an agency or run an internal marketing team: you have to add in the sales costs as well. This can, admittedly, get terrifying but is an awesome goal to shoot for in your

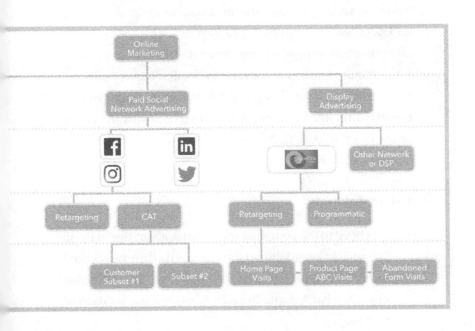

CFO/CEO blue sky analytics dream. But, again, this level of granular accounting in marketing performance analysis is unnecessary when a general cost per lead (CPL) and volume of leads can be used daily to manage and optimize your company's digital advertising successfully in the early stages. Again, the holy grail, final-stage KPI is cost per sale or cost per acquisition, but you need numbers to shoot for on a daily and weekly basis as well.

B. Web, Landing Page, and Creative Asset Design and creative optimization is essential. Any and every element of the creative used to drive interest—email, copy, images, landing pages, calls to action—must be tested against what is commonly referred to as a "Challenger." You must run A-B tests or Champion vs. Challenger tests to constantly be learning. Moreover, it is highly recommended to establish clone websites/landing pages for each module and for each sub-segment of customer you target.

C. Tracking and Reporting: You must be able to tie in the leads and sales (via the customer data in your CRM) to the dollar/advertisement/campaign that drove it. This requires a lead-level unique identifier at the time the lead or inquiry is "born" in your system. If you don't have this, you are spending money blindly. This information must be married with the query string or other data that is passed from the referring digital ad traffic source.

What does that mean?

•   You need to tell your data team things about the ad itself, like what keyword the person Googled before they clicked on your ad. Or if it was the yellow banner ad or the blue one. Or what website the ad was on and the location of that ad.

- You then need to marry this data with the lead record. For instance, Tom Donohoe became a lead in your CRM system on 1/1/2019 and he came from Bing and the keyword he came from was "Need awesome service from Acme Inc." and it came from this ad group in your Google Ads campaign.
- You then need to marry that collection of info with what happened to Tom Donohoe as a lead. Did he buy anything? Download a white paper and become a qualified sales lead? Did he request a call or a meeting? Did he become a client?
- That is the full stack of data based on a lead's life in your world that you need to understand and have the data to report on.

4. ESSENTIAL MARKETING TRACKING and REPORTING TECH ELEMENTS

Here are some granular things that must happen with each campaign to give you the data you need, as in the example above:

A. **Phone Tracking** = You must use unique 800 phone numbers on each ad and on landing pages so you can track performance to the campaign level. You will have many versions of the Canvas landing page for each module, each with a unique 800 phone number. Twilio is currently the best, cheapest, and most user-friendly SaaS platform to spin up unique 800 phone numbers.

B. **GTM** = Google Tag Manager ("GTM," reviewed in the Tech Primer above) or a similar tracking solution must exist across *every* page of your website and on *every* landing page. Adobe offers a solution as do many other options, though I'm partial to Google's. You need a way to track the actions of customers within your digital ecosystem, or else you can't collect and pass data and activity as effectively across your reporting or data location nodes (ex; digital ad channels, your CRM . . . places where data needs to come from). If your team is not using GTM, it is very likely they're not doing it correctly. It's like wearing pants to work. Sure you can work without pants, but it's pretty likely that you're not doing your best job in the office without them. Use of GTM is a very effective litmus test for executives to see if your teams are using the gold standard for data pass collection which is jargon for making sure info essential to you seeing ROI is being captured, passed to the right places, and stored where it can be used by smart people measuring ROI. Are you using GTM or a similar solution? Yes or no?

The next challenge is making sure that GTM is being used correctly. That's too granular for a CEO to get into so you should ask a qualified consultant to evaluate and give your team's GTM work a thumbs-up or -down. I promise that this will be the best Q&A time and money you've ever spent.

C. **ROI Reporting** = Again, at a high-level, your ideal flow and sequence of data collection and analysis should go like this for every single marketing campaign, online or offline. If it's not happening with every single campaign, stop and make sure you have this reporting and visibility, or you'll guarantee your team isn't using the right data to make profitable decisions.

- Start with the $$$ spent.
- Then pull in data about the ad itself such as the placement, ad type like Video #3 or a static image #7, and the keyword phrase a person Googled to find your ad.

- Add in the lead level data (like the zip code of the person, the type of product they inquired about, etc.).
- Finally, pull in the CRM Data, specifically the status of the lead (new, re-inquiry, and any lead status that may tell us if that person is moving through the sales funnel).
- And with all of this data married together, then and only then will you have a good bucket of aggregated data for your team to tell you every KPI you need to make good decisions, and for them to do the same.

D. Real time vs. Weekly manual. You do not have to have a fully automated data collection and analytics flow setup. You can do everything I've listed above manually. It sucks, and I've personally done this 100 or more times so I know the pain, but it's better than being in the dark about your real KPIs and ROI. And don't let anyone in your company tell you "we can't get the data." I've seen that answer be correct exactly never in companies likely in worse shape than yours. You can always get the data, even companies that use incredibly antiquated data repositories and reporting methods as straightforward as a chase scene in Indiana Jones.

CHAPTER 3

The C4

THE CORE FOUR: THE DAY ONE "BATTLEFIELD TRIAGE" DIGITAL MARKETING EVERY COMPANY MUST DO. EVERY COMPANY. RIGHT NOW.

OVERVIEW

BELOW ARE THE SIMPLE DIGITAL MARKETING things that, if your company isn't doing them—whether you make pencils or Ferraris or run a SaaS platform launched in 2020 or a 150-year-old manufacturing company—then your company is not doing good 21st Century-level marketing and is either losing money or leaving money on the table. Or both.

It is absolutely that simple.

The bad news? Nearly 80 to 90 percent of the time, these marketing campaigns simply don't exist, though we nearly always hear from the C-level executives that they have been *told* these things are happening at their company. And that's another issue entirely.

And sometimes when we *do* find that a company has deployed a few of these tactics, they aren't running them correctly and end up with bad ROI and a lack of confidence in digital advertising. It's pretty simple: Ten years ago, there were only a handful of things any company had to do in order to check the box on best practice digital marketing, and nearly all of those things could be done well in-house.

That is flat-out not even close to the reality in 2020 and beyond. These days we have five times more digital advertising channels that humans self-educate and purchase goods and services through (each of which can be very complex), three times more devices that we all own, and we have the ability to actually report on ROI by ad, by channel, by creative—thanks to advanced analytics platforms.

The chance is slim to none that any firm, without the help of a good agency or outside best practice consultancy, can say that they check off most of the items on this must-have list *and* manage and optimize each effectively. That's just life in the world of digital marketing that's now more than TWENTY years old!

The good news? Most of these strategies and campaigns we call the **Core Four** and **Advanced Eight** have three qualities which I love:

- They are relatively **CHEAP** in terms of media dollars to run each month.
- They are relatively **EASY** to create compared to some more advanced techniques.
- They are often some of the **MOST PROFITABLE** types of digital campaigns you can deploy.

The immediate Day 1 incentive for your company's marketing is to spend as little money as possible and create the most customers or leads using whatever campaigns represent "low hanging fruit" to establish the proof of concept for your marketing department. So I will introduce you to four strategies and eight specific tactics below that represent these high ROI/lower difficulty marketing budget-focused initiatives. But first, here are some other important details for these "Day 1, Phase 1" campaigns:

THE GOOD

- These campaigns will have a very low marketing cost for technology or media.
- They will be able to be executed by your employees so you don't have to hire an agency.
- They will be able to drive customers or leads in the short term and achieve quick wins.
- Their ROI, albeit at low budgets, is high and the risk is low.

THE BAD

- Such campaigns are rarely scalable activities, meaning that there is a point of diminishing returns for effort and a limited investment you can make.
- These rely heavily on an existing lead or customer database. For newer companies, this could present a problem.
- Some of these methods are meant to re-monetize or recapture prospective customers or leads that are already within the your brand's purview and, as such, if there are any limitations of reach (for instance, a certain type of individual) that may not in-line with the current database (e.g., you're launching a new product, a new location, want new types of clients, etc.), there is little that can be leveraged.
- You will likely be told by your marketing team that this stuff is already being done. But I will bet you ten free copies of this book that they are wrong and that, at minimum, they've checked the box and are doing a crappy job and leaving money and customers and efficiency on the table. This is not a guess. This is data based on a very large, statistically relevant sample set of companies in the B2B and HV B2C space.

THE CORE FOUR

So, these are the four short term/Day 1/Phase 1 tactics every company on Earth must do immediately.

Again, there is a significant amount of opportunity and profit in these low-hanging fruit Core Four tactics. That being said, they are *not* the only things you need to do in the long term and are certainly limited in terms of scaling your marketing and sales efforts. Each is low cost and high impact if your efforts are made in concert, with quality and contextual craftsmanship, and done consistently.

Here are some key points:

- If your firm already employs these baseline tactics, congrats. I'd guess 80 percent of CEOs and CMOs in High Value B2C and 90+ percent of B2B won't be able to check all these off their list.
- The short term (Day 1 => Day "Until The ROI Bleeding Stops") goal is to solve for the main marketing problems in your company, and to ensure the *baseline* tactics, landing pages, tracking/reporting, and ad platforms are being used, with the long-term goal of lowering overall Cost Per Acquisitions and providing strategic growth levers for customer generation.
- Notice I said "problems" and not "opportunities." Problems are things that are on fire, or are bleeding your money away into vapor and TPS reports of failure. Opportunities are enhancements to things that are going at least OK.
- I want to fix problems and then deal with more refined approaches.

CORE FOUR:

Every tactic listed below is very cheap and drives incredibly low cost per acquisition results.

Your team needs to do every single one of these things to be considered professional marketers. There is no excuse—zero, zip, nada—for not doing everything here.

1. **Tradename search engine advertising on Google and Bing**
   a. This is relatively cheap for every company in the world, from high volume B2C to heavy industry B2B or B2B SaaS platforms.
   b. If your marketing team is not doing this, consider firing your marketing team. Unless you are actively in Chapter 7 Bankruptcy, there is no excuse to not do this.

2. **Retargeting banner ads on social media and display ad networks**
   a. Site Visitor Retargeting
   b. 1-1 Lead Nurturing
      i. Aged leads
      ii. New Leads
      iii. Current Customers
3. **Landing pages—You *must* have them**
   a. If you are just using your homepage, you are setting money on fire.
   b. **The creative you are using to educate and compel your prospective customer to act must not suck. The landing pages** must be specific to the product or service, and based on the ad from which they came. Ideally, you should use video assets and client testimonials.
   c. **These pages** must follow standard best practice for direct response web design, employing features like unique 800 numbers, calls to action above the fold, and mobile-first design.
4. **Social media CAT targeting**
   a. Use the real email addresses for every new or aged lead in your database, or current customers if you are in an eCommerce environment.
   b. Target people on a 1-1 basis, meaning that you are only talking to those actual human beings on Facebook, and the match rate (meaning how many people out of 100 you upload will be able to be targeted) is around 40 percent for B2B and often more than 60 percent in B2C industries.
   c. This is an incredibly powerful and cheap targeting mechanism.

CORE #1: TRADENAME PAID SEARCH ENGINE MARKETING ("TN SEM") ON GOOGLE

It's simple. You want a *qualified* prospective high value B2C customer or prospective B2B client to see an advertisement every time someone Googles any combination of words which include something relevant to your company name, tradename or service mark, or trademark, or uniquely named product or service line:

- "IBM"
- "Bank of America loan"
- "Carnegie Mellon Tepper MBA application"
- "Hilton hotel reservations"
- "your company name"
- "Porsche 911 service center"
- "Delaware Credit Union checking acct"

It simply *does not matter* if your company already appears in what is called organic search (or the free listings—See Chapter 1 for the difference between SEM and SEO) when someone Googles your company name or the name of a trade/service-marked product you offer. *You must run tradename search engine advertising as well.* Why?

1. As of a report from 2019, when you run tradename advertising, there is an 89 percent incremental lift in the number of clicks you would receive without it. **This definitively means that if you run TN SEM correctly, you are likely to get about 90%**

more customers from this channel than relying on SEO alone. This is a fact and this is real data from real companies like yours. That is flat out crazy impressive (much higher than most people realize) considering the total cost and the type of response you get from these types of paid advertisement. If this was the only reason, you'd still do it. Most executives think that SEO by itself is good enough, and believe that if you run paid search ads (SEM), it will cannibalize your SEO. They are wrong to the tune of 89 percent.

2. You can control the exact landing page and ad copy/message a person sees for every unique product or service you offer better than if you use the general SEO result that Google will choose for you. You want to drive people to landing pages, not your homepage.

3. You force any of your competitors farther down the page or out altogether.

What we are talking about, using digital marketing industry acronyms, is **"TN SEM"** which comes from **Tradename Search Engine Marketing**.

Also, and per the snapshot of the percent use of each major search engine in the English-speaking world, if you take care of this on Google, that's nearly 90 percent of your market. Feel free to do the same thing with the other search platforms, but running TN SEM on Google Ads is a massive must-have.

And we all want to, quite simply, make sure that we serve up a relevant advertisement that we control—meaning the words used, as well as the links and phone numbers in the ad, and the exact website URL a person is sent to (hint: it's not going to be your homepage because that nearly always sets money on fire)—to the right person at the right time.

And per the notes regarding SEM versus SEO in Chapter 1, you cannot do that with SEO.

Moreover, we are going to specifically target and break down a TN SEM campaign into groups of recipients:

1. People Googling just the name of your company or a trademark or specific name of a service or product line. So, if your company's name is National Car Company, that person would be someone who Googled "National Car Co." or "National Car Company." What is essential is that you also do what is called negative matching using the tools available to you in Google and Bing. This means you install a list of words and, if they are included with your company's name in the Google search, we will not show that person your ad. The easiest example would be people looking for jobs. Most companies don't want to spend marketing dollars to market to people who are looking for jobs. So if someone Googled "National Car Company jobs," add "jobs" to that list of negative terms so the job-hunter does not see the ad.

    But this general targeting pool—often thrillingly called General Tradename Search in your media plan campaign—is as straightforward as it gets.

2. The additional TN SEM campaigns can be around your services or product lines. The difference is that the keyword phrases will include words or phrases that indicate someone wants to know about your company *and* a particular service or product line. The big deal here is that you're going to do a few things differently with the ads we show these people in that:

    a. The words we use in the ad actually talk about that specific product or service line!
    b. We are going to send them to a different URL! Not the homepage, but a page that speaks specifically to that product or service!
    c. You can include things called site links that are unique

to this service line, and unique phone numbers that call a different sales team, etc.

3. Other TN SEM campaigns can be around specific locations if your company has brick and mortar locations or if you're looking to service a specific market.

4. If you are a B2B company, you can get very specific if your product or service has success around a few verticals. For instance, equipment manufacturers or service companies who do a lot of business in the aerospace or automotive industries should have TN SEM campaigns specific to those industries.

GENERAL VS. OTHER TRADENAME SEARCH CAMPAIGNS

It is important to mention that executives and marketers need to be very careful about General TN SEM for companies whose names have very general words as a part of the brand such as:

- Universal Hardware Supply
- Bank of America
- Corporate Cleaning Solutions
- Heavy Equipment Company.

If your company has a very unique name, don't worry as much about this. But still be mindful of it.

Again, for those firms with very general words in the name of their company, do what is called exact match. There is a more advanced tactic called "cascading negatives" which we will not get into in this chapter. But never broad match, and certainly don't do a General TN SEM campaign if your company has a very general sounding name unless you set up an amazing list of negative match terms. Broad match, to quickly review, means that you'll target *everyone* who

Googles *any* of those words in *any* order. And, in practice, it's actually worse. Not to get too in the weeds, but the thing I just described is a fancy SEM category called Modified Broad Match. Real Broad Match is categorical . . . and that category is up to Google, not you. One example: you run a restaurant called Big Dog Café and you broad match that collection of words. Now you might show up in ads for a Golden Retriever's favorite food. If your company name is a collection of very general words, you cannot use broad match or else you'll end up targeting people who Google the word "equipment" or "bank," and thus waste your money with no ROI.

There are only a few dozen pairs of prefixes and suffixes and word pairs that—when you put them in any Google search—indicate that you want to show a person an ad for your company and they are very likely to be searching exactly for you.

As you build out new product or service lines, use the terms listed below as both prefixes and suffixes for key words for exact match (meaning you want that phrase *verbatim*).

Obviously, you will want to immediately build a database of negative match terms using bad examples of prior searches by people who have come to your site recently by way of the view in Google (for example) that lets you see what people had Googled when they saw your ad and clicked on it. Again, negative match terms are those that if any of the words appear in the search engine query on this list, your ad will not appear. Some basic and good examples of this are any words which indicate the person *is* looking for your company, but not to buy something or learn about your products as an interested prospective client:

- "careers"
- "job"
- "price list"
- "executive phone number"
- "address"

Then build out one advertising campaign using the directions below, and bid on these terms so your firm will show up when someone Googles what is commonly referred to as Tradename Search.

Oh, and this is the only time it is appropriate to want to always be ranked #1.

As an important tangent, If you know any marketer who still thinks it's important to "be ranked #1" in what is called non-Tradename search, throw them out of your office and call someone who knows more about digital marketing to help you. This is a serious suggestion. This means that the person is not doing ROI analysis by ad group or at the keyword level, and is using 10-year-old dangerous search engine strategy that has no place in your world.

But for Tradename Search, you do indeed want to be ranked #1 for the appropriate keyword phrases (with good negative matched keywords!) that have the name of your company or trademarked products or services in them.

A DEEPER DIVE

So using my company as an example, let's walk through a real Tradename Search campaign from a short window of time. Below is a screenshot of our Google Ads Tradename Search campaign from one of the ad groups (we get a little more fancy that you need to because, well, we are a digital marketing agency and we better be fancy):

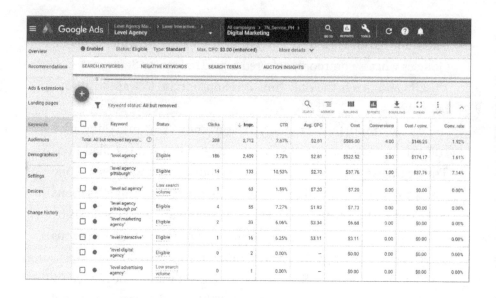

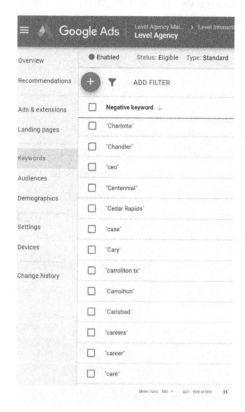

You cannot afford to lose visitors who search for these incredibly brand relevant and targeted terms for your products and services. But you also don't want to spend money on people looking for jobs, or competitors checking your prices, for example.

This is a screenshot of a handful of our negative keywords that we actively *do not* advertise when someone would Google the words "Level" and "Agency":

Even in this small sample, a dozen or so out of more than 900 (and still building each month as we see queries for people we don't want):

- I don't want to pay to advertise if they are looking for a "job" or "career"
- I don't want to appear in searches where we don't have an office such as Carrollton, Cedar Rapids or Charlotte, as wonderful as those places are! Why? Because even though we are not a local agency—we have massive national accounts with companies with scores of physical offices nationally and internationally— when someone Googles our name "Level Agency," they tend to be looking for an agency near where they live. A local shop. And if you're looking for a local shop that does not have an office in your hometown, we don't think you'll be a good lead because we only have offices in a few cities (and they, of course, are not on this list).
- I don't want people looking for me, the CEO. Or my President. Or my VPs. Or my interns. Those queries are often done by staffing firms or people looking to poach my people or sell me stuff. And I don't want to pay money each time they click on a paid advertisement.

If you took a look under my company's TN SEM hood, you would also see the following:

- My company, called Level Agency, used to be called Level Interactive. So we actively bid on that keyword phrase as well.
- You can see how we've broken this campaign into a few categories with a few examples of keywords we're bidding on:
  - ° A General campaign, which is just variations of our company name with a heavy list of negative terms we do not want to have ads appear for, such as (negative words in bold):

- ✓ "Level Agency careers"
- ✓ "Level Agency executives"—a common query by sales people looking to sell us stuff
- ✓ "Level Five Agency"—another company with a similar name that is *not* my company
  - ° Product and Service line specific campaigns. These are a combination of our company name plus the names or descriptions of the main services we offer:
    - ✓ Digital Advertising
      - • "Level Agency online advertising"
      - • "Level media buying"
      - • "Level Agency digital media"
        - ° Call Center Support
          - • "Level Agency call centers"
          - • "Level telephone sales support"
        - ° Web Design and Development
          - • "Level website design"
          - • "Level landing page optimization"
  - ° Location Specific Campaigns—While we are running TN SEM campaigns nationally, we are being more aggressive with our service line (see above) TN SEM campaigns in specific cities where we have offices or a nice client concentration:
    - ✓ Los Angeles
    - ✓ Phoenix/Scottsdale
    - ✓ Pittsburgh and the Tri-State area around our headquarters
    - ✓ Charleston, South Carolina
    - ✓ Washington DC / Baltimore / Tysons Corner, Virginia
    - ✓ Miami / Ft. Lauderdale
    - ✓ Denver
    - ✓ Dallas
    - ✓ Other major U.S. cities.

Again, this is *only for my company*. We are a B2B services company. Your company is *very* different, so your TN SEM campaigns—outside of the General TN SEM campaign—should reflect the unique types of work your company does, products or services you offer, areas or industries you work within.

HOW TO TELL YOUR TEAM HOW TO BEGIN IF YOU ARE NOT DOING TN SEM TODAY

I will say it 100 times over if I have to: You *must* run TN SEM if you are not already doing so. Every company. In every industry. Selling or doing anything.

One important caveat: you should not do this if your company already has a Google Ads account. Companies pointing to the same domain with two accounts is a gray area in Google's advertising terms—especially if you inadvertently (or intentionally) begin bidding on the same term and show up in the same auction twice between the two accounts—that's a big red flag that can get you perma-banned.

To create your campaign, head to https://ads.google.com and find the "Get started now" button, and sign up for a Google Ads account. It used to be called Google AdWords and is the same thing. Once you're logged in, click the "Create your first campaign" button.

1. Select your campaign type and the name you want to call it. Choose the campaign type—we will recommend the "Search Network only" option—and then give it a name. Don't check the box for "Include search partners" because that starts advertising off the www.google.com website and that would be for more aggressive campaigns.
2. Choose the geographic location where you'd like to advertise for your company. Pick countries, cities and regions.

3. Choose your "bid strategy," and set what you think should be your daily budget. If you're just starting and if this is just for tradename search, you can put in $100 unless your company is a Fortune 1000. I will still contend that you should never limit a well-built TN SEM campaign by budget. If it is built well, literally run it wide open. Change the default bid strategy to "I'll manually set my bids for clicks" which won't just run for impressions but gives you a nice middle ground on the target you're shooting for instead of aiming only for new leads. You could start by selecting automated bidding and set the bid position to 1st position, as I have seen used with some success, but the risk is that your team will rely on auto-bidding for the long term and in more complex SEM campaigns, and that could lead to trouble.

    • Your daily budget is the maximum that Google is authorized to charge you per day. For TN SEM, I'm telling you that unless you're a massive Fortune 1000 company, you're not going to spend that much.
    • Set your daily budget a little lower for non-tradename accounts (which we'll cover in Chapter 4 under the more advanced SEM strategies) with a number so that if you make a mistake like forgetting to send clicks to a website you won't lose all of your money. But, again, for TN SEM, you can set a pretty high daily number.

4. Now follow the very easy steps that Google Ads has laid out to create your first ad group (that's where you break down your company into different service lines or cities where you have an office, etc.) and write a few different ads using a few different ways to talk about your company's value proposition.

    Here are the quick data points of the ads that you're going to create:
    • Headline 1 is up to 30 characters of text

- Headline 2 is up to 30 characters of text
- Headline 3 is up to 30 characters of text
- Description 1 is up to 90 characters of text
- Description 2 is up to 90 characters of text
- The last line is your main URL or a specific landing page that you've made for your company.

5. Insert your keywords into the keyword area. Use the keywords you have built from both the name of your company and the tradename of your service or product. Paste in your keywords and see what is returned.

6. For non-tradename search campaigns, you really need to set your maximum cost-per-click pretty high. But for these basic and very low volume and low hanging fruit tradename campaigns, you can be very aggressive to ensure you'll be ranked #1. This, again, is the only type of search campaign where you want to be at the very top. That type of method for other campaigns that are not surrounding the name of your company will get you in a ton of trouble and guarantee you'll waste a ton of money.

   - For non-tradename searches, if your company can afford $50 per day instead of $5,000, it's better to bid on low-cost keywords so that your ad can be seen by as many people as possible. Due to the limitations of any budget, if you're going after high-priced keywords, you'll exhaust your budget quickly and your ads will only be seen part of the day rather than for a full 24 hours.
   - For tradename searches, again, I would advise you to bid at the maximum suggested bid to place #1, and that might be $10 or more (not that you'll end up paying that much).

7. Enter your billing information, because you need to pay Google for every time someone clicks on your amazing ad.

Your ads will start showing as soon as you confirm your payment information.

https://support.google.com/partners/answer/3153810?hl=en

This is a link to the "Help" article that links out to all of the trainings. Google doesn't let you link directly to the training because you have to be signed in, so make certain you first create an account for your company.

Use the https://adwords.google.com/ko/KeywordPlanner/Home and insert any prefixes or suffixes, in addition to product-specific terms, and Google will produce hundreds of keywords to use in your Tradename Search Engine Marketing.

CORE #2: RETARGETING BANNER ADS VIA GOOGLE AND SOCIAL MEDIA (FACEBOOK)

Showing someone who has visited any of your web properties—your website, landing pages, microsites, blogs—a banner ad that is relevant to the content or product or topic of the page that they visited is one of the cheapest and most cost-effective ways to get that person back to your world and convert them into a customer. You can do this through many channels and advertising platforms. If you are starting out your company's digital marketing journey, I recommend that you use only Google and Facebook because of their massive reach, effective targeting and optimization options, and ease of use, and you'll be using these platforms for other things anyway.

GOOGLE

While banner ads, or display ads as they are called in the marketing world, can be purchased many different ways, the platform which by far offers the best combination of easy use for a novice, best targeting options, the best cost structure (cost per click vs. cost per 1000 impressions), and the best breadth and depth of ad inventory is Google Ads. Yes, the same platform where you just built out your Tradename Search campaigns is the same interface and advertising channel where you can buy banner ads.

There are platforms which offer greater targeting, enhanced media placement and strategy options, but they are significantly more sophisticated to operate and require complex contracts and vendor partnerships to be established.

Google's banner ad platform—which was/is called the Google Display Network (or GDN for short)—is as self-service as it gets, and many digital agencies calling themselves advanced display advertising vendors kind of cheat by only using GDN vs. the more complex systems (Demand Side Platforms called DSP's for short, explained in Chapter 1, as a more robust way to buy banner ads). These agencies get away with it because of the quality of this platform. While GDN doesn't have the reach of the DSPs, its reach is more than adequate for these purposes.

Also, if a digital marketing agency is charging you a lot of money to run banner ads for you and they are not using a DSP, you should find a better agency.

Most importantly, here are the reasons why banner ad retargeting via Google is one of the four in the Core Four's must-have elements in digital advertising for all companies:

1. It's surprisingly cheap and easy to set up.
2. It is like targeting very dumb ducks in a very small barrel— you are only showing ads to people who have already visited your website.
3. It's very effective at driving a good ROI because of the low ad cost and the perfect audience—the people who have already been to your company website and/or landing pages.
4. You can get very granular and targeted and show people ads that are relevant to a specific product or service because you know the web page they visited and you don't have to just show them a general ad for your company.
5. . . . and it's incredibly cheap . . . which is worth saying twice.

GENERAL STEPS TO LAUNCH

Step 1: Use the banner ad portion of Google Ads.

Step 2: Create product or service specific banner ads that are engaging (hint: videos or rich media vs. static image) and for which you can use any existing creative already on your website (e.g., that "explainer" video about why your company is great?? Use parts of that for an ad!).

Step 3: Cookie people who visit all the different pages of your website—beyond just the homepage. Have different ads for each section, service line, product category, and location of your company.

Step 4: Serve the ads on this Google display network with a frequency cap of no more than three so you're not ticking people off (that means each cookied person isn't seeing more than three of your ads every day).

It's cheap and a very good ROI.

Below is a screen shot showing the familiar Google Ads interface with the banner ad campaign called "retargeting display" (our name, but you can call your campaign whatever you want). You can see how well it integrates with the Google search campaigns you just built, and view some examples of the banner ad types it can use (static image and an animated HTML 5 ad).

DETAILED TACTICAL EXECUTION

The most important thing is to "do" retargeting banner ads. If you're not running them, you're not even in the game of trying to do 21st Century Marketing. But what about doing them *well*?

In Chapter 4, we'll talk about more advanced versions of the campaigns listed here in the Core Four—the search engine, social network, and (here) the baseline display advertising that you simply must be running if you have a company based on Planet Earth in this century. But that's not what the Core Four are about.

These Core Four things, including display ad retargeting, are the baseline tactics in digital that are low cost, high ROI, and fairly straightforward to set up, often not requiring a marketing agency. So while the first point (the steps listed above) are how to set up the general retargeting campaign, the next piece is how to do it beyond a Fisher-Price level. And it's neither that hard to deploy nor is it really that strategically complex.

The creative strategy that follows will get you a good, effective banner ad retargeting set up with a bit of nuance and targeting sophistication:

1. Understand that retargeting someone (e.g., showing them a banner ad) who has visited the homepage of your website but no other pages is going to justify a *different* banner ad than someone who:

    a. Went to your homepage
    b. Then went to one of your main product or service pages or one of your location pages
    c. Then went to your pricing page

2. In the example above, you need to know which pages they've seen, and then put some logic to it. Your marketing team can do this using code that's available in Google Ads (there are

more complex ways to do it, but this is the most simple) and laying out in a matrix of Who Sees What Ad based on the page(s) they've visited.

3. As an example, if you have different products or services, make 100 percent sure you have a banner ad suite for each one of them.

4. Different locations or pages on your site that are for very different experiences or consumer search behaviors? Yup, make a banner ad suite for those, too.

CREATIVE EXECUTION

While you're not going to be the one designing the banner ads, you need to understand that the baseline acceptable banner ad suite consists of:

1. The following ad sizes are the least number of sizes your team needs to churn out for EACH banner ad—together called a "banner ad suite/set"—and no, you cannot use one size for another. Your team must build one for each size listed here. Do not cheat and have an ad platform like Google automatically resize them. That makes them look horrible and you'll be doing your company more harm than good:

   a. 160x600
   b. 300x250
   c. 336x280
   d. 728x90
   e. 300x600
   f. 320x100 (mobile)
   g. 320x50 (mobile)

   Yes, there are other sizes. No, they are not served as much as the ones above (and I'd argue that to achieve the baseline in banner ad retargeting competency, you don't need them).

2. You must have your team design both static and dynamic HTML 5 ads. Static means they don't show any animation or any movement. They're the type of ads that are served if the website where your customer is viewing them doesn't play nice with the dynamic ads. Dynamic ads have specifications to them (file size and the number of times/length that the animation will play), but just make sure your design team isn't actively trying to sabotage you. Make sure that they do the following:

    a. Look good.
    b. Have a clear call to action that is the biggest thing your eyeballs notice when you look at the ad.
    c. Send people to the right web page or landing page.

3. This last point is most important. Let me suggest two ways to run banner ad retargeting. One is easy, and will not really do your company much good. The other is still block-and-tackling in the world of banner ad retargeting, but is best practice for a Core Four baseline level of digital marketing competency.

    d. EXAMPLE PATH ONE = You only have one banner ad set for your company and you show every person who visits your site the same banner ad set regardless of where they went, and you send them back to your homepage.
    e. EXAMPLE PATH TWO = You have an intelligent number of banner ad sets for your company based on the number of product categories or services you offer, locations, etc. So when someone sees a banner ad, it's because they went to a very specific handful of pages within your site. Moreover, when they click on one of these ads, they are not taken to the homepage, but instead to a web page that is very content-specific and very good at turning

visitors into leads and customers who act. Make sure you're trying to follow Example Path Two.

One important caveat: If you only have 5 or 10 people visiting some of your product pages every month, it's probably not worth building out creative efforts for them at this stage, because the audience size isn't big enough to impress against.

Consider at least 100 visitors per month in your segmentation minimum requirement, which means that if you try to over-segment, and you don't have the audience size to support it, you'd have put in a lot of time and, more importantly, money to build a thing that will literally do nothing for you.

But we'll assume that most of the people reading this book have monthly website traffic figures high enough where this is not a concern.

FACEBOOK

The delightful reality of the larger and more profitable social media platforms for direct response advertisers, namely Facebook and little/big brother Instagram, is that while these platforms share the exact same backend interface for running paid advertisements, they tend to change the user interface and the targeting options often (and even very often, if they are getting destroyed in the court of public opinion and/or real U.S. or international courts to regulate what they can and cannot or should and should not offer to advertisers like us in terms of targeting people).

This means that the directions I give for creating accounts—showing the first few steps on how to set up a campaign and link that to your corporate credit card, what goals to get—all of these things change at least once a year if not more and, as such, the visual aids that I want to provide (as I did with Google, above) to lay out the whole process will likely be wrong by the time you read this . . . or soon thereafter.

But the final steps—those clicks you make after you have someone on your team set up a Campaign (Facebook's top level category of an advertisement tranche) and an Ad Set (the equivalent of an Ad Group in Google)—I'll show you which are the incredibly easy steps to using Facebook and Instagram's massive reach of billions of users and showing them ads if they visited your website (retargeting).

So here is the high level implementation plan for banner ad retargeting on social media via the biggest channels, Facebook and Instagram:

When building your campaign, make sure to set your campaign objective to "Conversion"

Create New Campaign ▼	
Campaign Name	Remarketing Campaign
Buying Type	Auction ▼
Campaign Objective	⬤ Conversions ▼
Split Test ❶	◯
Campaign Budget Optimization ❶	◉
Campaign Budget ❶	Daily Budget ▼ $100.00
	Actual amount spent daily may vary. ❶

Select the conversion event that equals a lead on your website:

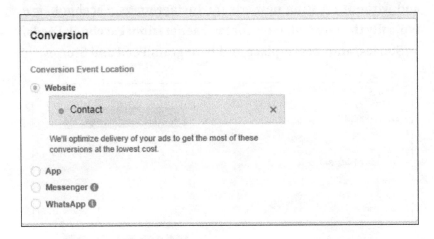

Select the remarketing audience you want to use from the "Custom Audiences"

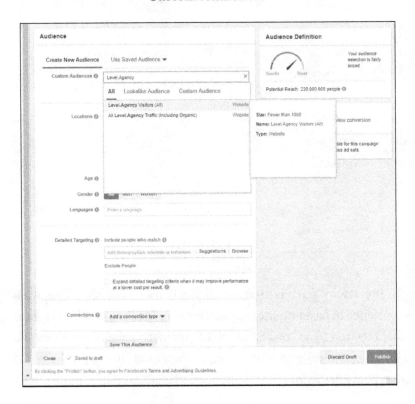

Cut down the number of placements to the five that, as a default and without creating new ads for Instagram vs. Facebook, are typically the most effective for lead generation: Facebook Feeds, Stories, and Marketplace and Instagram Feed and Stories.

The tricky part is that you'll need to direct someone with experience in baseline site tagging (putting Facebook and Instagram code referred to as "pixels" on all of your web pages so you can see who goes where) and a bit of experience with using the backend advertising platform of these sites (which, again, change quite often)

to allow Facebook to identify as Custom Audiences specific groups of people who have visited certain pages in your website. While it is not in practice that difficult, that would be the one element that can trip up entry-level digital advertisers. Most importantly, harness the biggest advantage of digital advertising (again, targeting people surgically) and create several categories of Custom Audiences. People who reach the web page or landing page for Product123? They should be in their own Custom Audience if that pool of people is large enough to make sense.

One quick note of good news: once you have this tracking pixel placed all over your site—every single page—the tool that Facebook and Instagram uses to build out these Custom Audiences (the activity is called "audience building") doesn't require you to use different pixels on different pages. Just put the same code on every page and you can use the ad platforms to create these different audiences. Again, it could be everyone who visited the pricing page or the Product123 page, or your location page in Manhattan's Lower East Side; it just takes one pixel across your whole website. There is one piece of code to rule them all, which makes your life a bit easier from a technology deployment standpoint.

It also means that if you have a larger company or are working with any agency, it's important for you to know (a) that this type of incredibly granular audience building and targeting is easy, and (b) your teams better be doing it because for professional marketers and agencies, this should be child's play.

WHAT HAPPENS AFTER THE CLICK IN RETARGETING ADS?

Lastly, it is essential for search engine (Google to start) and social networks (Facebook and Instagram to start) retargeting ad campaigns to not only use banner ads (please remember to use rich media ads for Google and video-based ads if you can for the social networks!), but also to drive people to websites that are relevant to exactly the web pages they visited on your website.

Did they visit your homepage and then go to Product123's page? Then you should show them an ad that is about Product123 and, when clicked, it takes them to a website specific to Product123!

As I've said before, the core magic and power of digital advertising and 21st Century Marketing is the ability to target people surgically. And this does not just begin and end with the advertisements and ad channels themselves. This is absolutely relevant to the websites they visit.

What kind of websites? We've mentioned before in Chapter 1 about Landing Pages. Now that we've introduced yet again the idea of a landing page as the final step in digital advertising that allows you to target a specific person and their specific interest surgically, now's a perfect time to talk about the #3 tactic in the Core Four.

CORE #3: LANDING PAGES— EVERY COMPANY SHOULD HAVE THEM

Other than driving the best prospective clients and customers to your company's web presence for a cost per click that backs into a good cost per lead/sale, the most important thing is what happens *after* they click.

I can't tell you how many marketers—giant, famous, expensive agencies and huge internal marketing teams—focus most of their efforts on Ninja-grade search engine advertising (and other channels) and either *ignore* the websites customers are sent to, or *leave* the work to the client to figure out.

And very often, this means that everyone that is driven to a company's website ends up on the worst page in the world: **YOUR HOMEPAGE**.

If you want to destroy your ROI with your digital marketing efforts, please keep driving people to your homepage.

If you would like to do a better job with turning money into new customers, think: LANDING PAGES.

WHAT ARE LANDING PAGES?

- Landing pages are "flat" websites—meaning the viewer can't really jump around a ton, but there is just enough information and rich media and value proposition of your company to get someone to the next step of the conversation.
- Whereas your main website has 6-10 different jobs (communicate with new customers, current customers, employees, candidates, stakeholders, press/media, etc.), the

landing page has only one: Convert a visitor into someone taking *action*. That can be a lead submitted, request for more info, a chat, or just a phone call.

- Simply, a landing page's job is simply to not drop the ball when it comes to converting any paid web traffic, meaning targeted visitors you want to get to your website.

WHY USE LANDING PAGES?

As we covered in Chapter 1, sending paid advertising visitors to a more tailored experience in accordance with what the user is seeking means more of those visitors will turn into actions—phone calls or leads or downloads, and eventually sales.

Additionally, it is essential that your company implement a comprehensive landing page testing strategy that will identify which elements of a landing page users engage with most, and which items will lead to improved customer generation in paid advertising efforts.

WHY LANDING PAGES ARE IMPORTANT (AND WHAT SEO URLS AND EFFORTS CANNOT DO):

- Well-tailored content and sales experience—the right message shown to a specific human driven from specific keywords or social media profiles (so you know what they most likely want or need from your company)
- Fewer distractions in navigating the page *en route* to interacting with your sales funnel (e.g., login button for current clients)
- Serves one purpose: to convert visitors into prospective clients/ make a sale. Things like above-the-fold copy are essential, which is impossible when driving to a untailored page on your website.

- Remove extraneous sections that only confuse users to get lost in pre-and post-lead submission.

Below is a quick real-world example of landing page conversion results that came about through iterative landing page tests for one client. *These results are not exceptional, btw.* With good Homepage => Landing Page migration of your current traffic and sales path, you should see noticeable improvements in click to lead/action conversion rates, which positively affects the most important KPI in our world: Cost Per Acquisition.

These results come from:

✓ 100 percent of visitors tested
✓ Unique ads and landing pages with messaging tweaked toward products, campaigns, demographics, and more
✓ Iterative testing strategy that takes the guesswork out of ad and landing page optimization
✓ Quantifiable data to better tailor creative messaging to specific audiences.

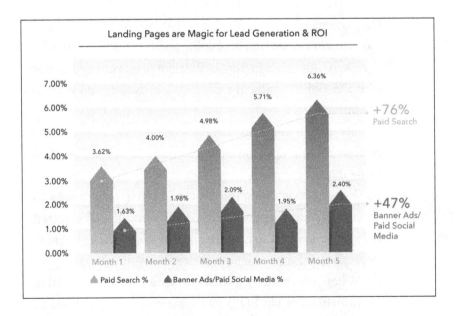

Again, these results aren't rare. We are not curing disease or turning water into '82 Bordeaux here at my agency. We focus on the whole process: from spending money to serve an impression all the way through a lead being born and on to a customer being created. You need to do this as well in your company and customer journey. Do not forget: the customer journey includes steps in the middle, after seeing the ad and before becoming a lead, the crux of which is the landing page experience.

When you, as a B2B or High Value B2C company, move from driving paid traffic from your homepage to tailored landing pages, you're going to see a real step change in your click-to-lead conversion rates. And when you demand that your marketing team own the full journey from dollar being spent to a sale being made and every step in between, good ROI happens.

Below are some general wireframes and real examples (again, using my agency as a simple example) that you can use to begin to understand what the best practice UX/UI is in the world of landing pages.

Keep in mind that:

- Our landing pages are not perfect. They are just a few out of a thousand examples online of doing good stuff and putting the right web experience in front of the right prospective customer with the right creative message with a data-driven path to becoming a lead.
- We are a B2B service business—and every industry and customer path, especially in when you compare B2B to High Value B2C, is different.
- You'll need to understand that a landing page needs to encourage a prospective client or customer, a well-targeted and relevant *visitor*, to become someone who wants to know more about your product or service. Ask yourself:
  ✓ What information (words or video or downloadable information via PDF) can I provide these visitors to

encourage them to want more from my sales team?

✓ What user experience makes sense for the type of person I'm driving here? Are they often individuals with MBAs and PhDs? Perhaps those people innately demand more content and a more in-depth user path than other consumer categories.

✓ What elements are immediately or quickly visible on a cell phone from your landing page that allow a visitor to connect with your company in the way they want to reach out? Is that a unique 800 phone number? A lead gen/request for information form? A chat feature? Are you driving many different types (ages, for example) of customers to this one landing page and therefore should have all three of these contact methods present?

Ask these types of questions as you build out your landing pages and you'll begin to treat your website as the essential first step in a visitor becoming a customer.

LANDING PAGES EXAMPLE:

Below is a real-world example of a B2B landing page that my agency uses. Notice the following best-practice elements that every landing page should have in B2B or High Value B2C:

1. Multiple calls to action above the fold. This means that there are multiple different ways (in this example, three) for a prospective customer to reach out and communicate with your firm:

   a. a unique 800 number specific for the ad channel and campaign that drove the traffic,

   b. a lead gen form, often called a request for information ("RIF") and, in this case, a progressive form that only shows a few fields to fill out before progressively moving to the next set of questions. This increases response rates and gives the marketing team more options to connect and remarket the person if they only fill out the first set of data points and then drop off.

c.   a chat feature which pops up after a certain fixed amount of time There can be other calls to action, such as a link to a unique email address, but using these three are standard best practice for high price point, non-eCommerce items. Being "above the fold" means that you can visually see each of them without scrolling down both on your desktop or mobile device.

2.   A background image and/or other images that are relevant to the product or service

3.   The page is mobile optimized, meaning it looks good on a handheld device

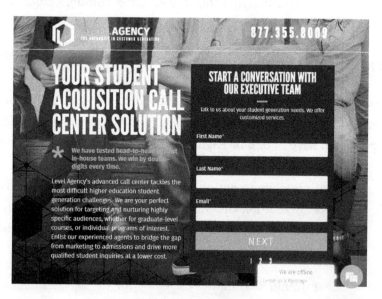

Below is another version of a landing page that my agency uses for B2B using a slightly different approach. Instead of asking for a prospective customer's information upfront, we offer some insights or

industry information and, in exchange, we ask only a few questions. This is what is called offering up "gated content," where some value is given, typically a white paper or case study or something that would be of academic or professional value to the prospective client and, in exchange, they provide us with a limited piece of information to follow up.

These gated content experiences in landing pages are typically best used for non-consumer goods and products and services that have very long sales cycles and are fairly complex in nature (ex: B2B SaaS companies' product lines).

Regardless of what level of information you show your prospective audience, make sure that (a) you are driving prospective clients and customers to targeted landing pages with surgical content tailored to the specific advertisement you are running, and (b) you are using best practice UX/UI design concepts.

CORE #4: SOCIAL NETWORK LEAD NURTURING VIA FACEBOOK

We have already reviewed the key aspects of paid social network advertising, primarily on Facebook, Instagram, and LinkedIn. If you need to review the nuances of these platforms, go re-read the sections in Chapter 1 above.

The most essential social network tactic, a must-have for every company in the world, is using email addresses to target specific humans who are already in your social media database. Facebook calls this "CAT" campaigns, short for Custom Audience Targeting.

Simply put, you are going to take every email address in your database and you are going to upload that list into Facebook (which also owns Instagram), and you are going to show ads to *only* those human beings that belong to those email addresses.

Much like retargeting display ads (Core #2), this is like shooting very dumb ducks in a very small barrel.

Again, much like direct mail, you are putting a very specific message in front of specific human beings using the digital advertising platform that powers Facebook and Instagram. It used to be called Facebook Power Editor and is now just called Facebook Ads Manager. This incredibly powerful platform can be used in-house. The step-by-step guide below can get an in-house person started with a basic effort known as Facebook Custom Audience Targeting ("FB CAT").

You can target the following things in Facebook and Instagram, but this FB CAT option is very inexpensive and very powerful. Here are some additional data points on this must-have digital campaign for every company in the world:

- This is not for people who don't know about your product, service or company. Technically, this tactic falls under what marketing calls "nurturing," but it is the single most exceptional means to do the following:
  - ✓ Take people currently in your database who have never bought anything from your or have never become clients and turn them into clients
  - ✓ Take current clients and make them spend more money or engage with your company and sales team/account team more
- The only piece of information you need are email addresses. Yes. That's it. Nothing more.
- This is so much more effective than sending email campaigns, and it would be funny if it wasn't so sad how many companies have been running declining-in-efficacy email campaigns for years but don't run Facebook CAT using the exact same email list.
- Much like TN SEM and Retargeting Display, these Facebook CAT campaigns are *cheap.*
- Much like TN SEM and Retargeting Display, these Facebook CAT campaigns are *incredibly effective* and have an amazing ROI.
- Every company in the world selling or doing *anything* should run Facebook CAT tomorrow.

Here is a quick snapshot of some of the general targeting options in Facebook. Note how easy it is to find the option to use email addresses to target people one-on-one on Facebook:

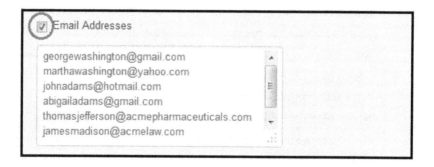

Facebook Audience Targeting Options

There are many options for narrowing down your audience:

- **Geography/Location**
  - Country, City, DMA, Zip Code
- **Demographics**
  - Age, Gender, Language, Education Level, Job Title, Company, etc.
- **Device**
  - Mobile or Desktop
- **Interests/Connections**
  - Content people share, pages they like, etc.
- **Behaviors**
  - Target purchasing behaviors and buyer personas based on third party data analysis of activity outside Facebook.
  - Ex. coupon users, outdoor enthusiasts, soccer moms, etc.

Audience Definition

Your audience selection is fairly broad.

Specific — Broad

Audience Details:
- Location:
  - United States: Washington, DC (Hagrstwn) (DMA)
- Age:
  - 35 - 55
- Gender:
  - Female
- Placements:
  - News Feed on mobile devices or Instagram Feed
- People Who Match:
  - Interests: Cooking

☑ Email Addresses

georgewashington@gmail.com
marthawashington@yahoo.com
johnadams@hotmail.com
abigailadams@gmail.com
thomasjefferson@acmepharmaceuticals.com
jamesmadison@acmelaw.com

CREATIVE EXECUTION

Once you have created some Facebook CAT campaigns targeting different tranches of your existing lead database, it is beyond essential that you embrace the following facts:

1. The creative message—the call to action, the content, the image/videos, the story, your company's value proposition— that you used to *create* this lead must be different from the creative message you use to *nurture* this lead as the prospects move through your sales funnel.

2. Because there is no single action, you need a lot *more* creative than you had in your arsenal to create the lead in the first place. Think about: turning a random person into a lead is a singularity. They were advertised "at," you drove them to your landing page, and they became a lead. Now, while this journey technically doesn't happen in the same 5-minute span—there is a massive conversation about up-funnel, pre-lead-gen brand advertisement attribution (see Chapters 2 and 4—attribution models)—the journey from lead to sale requires even more variety of creative messaging to take this person down your sales funnel.

So what does this mean in practice when you need rubber to hit the road? Here are the things you must tell your teams to make sure they're not just recycling the *same* creative that made the lead in the first place.

TACTICAL EXECUTION

-   With the initial creation of the lead, you had some nice variety of ads on search engines and social networks—and across other channels—that hopefully spoke to a unique audience that you targeted intentionally with a *tailored* message specific to their needs telling them why your product or service is better than sunshine and sliced bread.
-   Good work! You did your job and made a lead.
-   Now this lead wants to know a lot more about why they should take a big leap, much bigger than just giving you their name and email address. If they become more than a lead, they're going to have to talk and interact with someone in your company.

This is a huge step in the emotional gestation of a customer and one that, to borrow a term from mechanical physics, requires a larger bit of activation energy. Starting a car rolling from a full stop takes more force than keeping it moving along after it's going.

Marketing is the opposite.

Keeping a lead moving through the sales cycle requires much more creative effort than making the lead in the first place.

- So, take all of the value propositions and the common objections for that type of customer (remember, you have segmented these leads into different categories, whether it's by type of product they need or type of consumer they are) and start creating social media ads around those.
- Start a multi-step package of creative messages and show them to an audience, best-case scenario, via this Facebook CAT method, in a logical series. At worst, just make sure you target these segmented CAT audiences with more than one message, more than one value proposition, and more than one solution to their common objections.
- In ads, video is more powerful than a static image.
- Once they click on an ad, ask yourself where is this person who is *already a lead* going to go? Another landing page? If so, what will it say? Will it be awesome testimonials of your company's current clients? Something to bolster your legitimacy and value proposition? Dream it, you executive dreamer, you.

Do this, and your Facebook CAT lead nurturing efforts are going to help make your sales efforts significantly more effective.

CHAPTER 4

C4 vs. A8

THE ADVANCED EIGHT: YOUR LONG-TERM STRATEGY IN CUSTOMER GENERATION. BEYOND DIGITAL AND INTO FULL STACK MARKETING

MANY PEOPLE THINK THAT I HATE traditional advertising like TV, print, radio, and billboards or same-for-generations marketing tactics like tradeshows and PR because I was born into the world of marketing when digital was the new, shiny object.

Man, they're wrong.

The reason I despise these pre-historic channels is because they typically blow through your budget with near-zero accountability. Headed to that tradeshow and dropping $40,000 on a 20x20-foot booth with airfare and hotels? Why? Because your competitors are doing it? Because you've always done it that way and if it ain't broke, don't fix it? Because ol' Henry and ol' Gil down in sales would throw a fit if you didn't go?

No, although nothing listed above is a good reason to attend an expensive conference.

No, the reason I dislike the overreliance on, or eternal attendance at, the same tradeshows year after year is because rarely have CEOs done the baseline analysis to track back leads—qualified leads that turned into new customers—to that event. They might ask if any leads came from an event, but that's not even close to doing a cost benefit ROI analysis and match that head to head against other line items. That's why I tend to empirically hate tradeshows and discourage my clients and friends from just doing the same events year after year, generation after generation. It's less because of the thing itself and much more because of how poorly it's focused on profitability and lead generation.

Do I hate TV because it was invented nearly 100 years ago and by a guy named Philo T. Farnsworth??

No, although every part of that sentence is amazingly true.

I hate TV advertising because it's incredibly overpriced compared to its customer generation outcomes. Because TV rarely has quantifiable definitive sales metrics, and instead touts worthless Nielsen ratings that don't put meat on the table. Most importantly, TV creative is beyond expensive to deploy well unless you're filming your 60-second spot using your cell phone, the way they made "The Blair Witch Project."

But I never hate old-school, traditional sales approaches just because they're old.

I hate them only when they have one of the three following properties, which they often do:

- Bad ROI / massively overpriced vs. the revenue they drive
- You can't track and quantify the ROI, leads, or sales
- You can't optimize your creative or tactics based on data

But do you know what I *love*?

Traditional tactics and behaviors that *work*, that are direct drivers of results and revenue, that use data to get smarter and better ROI and results, direct leads and demonstrable customers. That's what I love.

Let's talk about these things and how they can work hand in hand with your newfound digital savvy.

THE LONG-TERM, FULL STACK STRATEGY IN SALES AND MARKETING

After you are 100 percent sure the Core Four are running at your company—and only after—you'll know your firm has established a 21st Century Marketing baseline through ROI-focused digital marketing because you're getting some quantifiable and optimizable lead flow established. And when you know that the foundation has been built well and is up and running, it's appropriate to begin thinking about *what's next.*

You need to have other channels and tactics, both online and offline, working in concert. Why? Because while the Core Four digital campaigns reviewed in Chapter 3 are the simplest, lowest hanging fruit customer generation tactics that work for every company in the world and can be built fairly easily, and they are limited in scale. Some next steps for what to do after the Core Four are, indeed, traditional methods as well as new twists on digital channels.

After you've established the baseline, 24/7/365 low hanging fruit lead pipeline, we want the following:

- New lead flow and customer generation that is scalable with higher limits to points of diminishing returns than the Core Four
- Direct, traditional marketing methods that sync in financial and data-driven harmony with your new 21st Century Core Four framework.
- More options of where to invest your marketing budget and the time/salaries of your employees and/or agency fees. The more options you have across your product and service lines,

the more able your team will be to lower Cost Per Acquisitions, especially for those sectors or customer profiles or service/product lines or locations that have difficulty driving new leads and customers, and where you need to swing at a ton of new and different pitches to try and connect with new customers and a recipe for scalable lead flow.

The primary reason to do some of these things isn't because you'd like to make sure that salespeople and telephones still have a place in the world—it's profit scale, and efficiency. The methods below are both old school and new school, phone based and internet driven, but they all rely upon tried and true marketing theories that, when working alongside best practice digital marketing, provide the following:

- Good ROI. Well priced when compared to the revenue they drive.
- You can definitively track and quantify the ROI, leads, or sales lift or improvement from these specific things.
- You can optimize your creative approach and tactics based on the same data you used to optimize your digital advertising lead generation funnel.

Again, we are certainly not talking about most go-to campaigns you'll see in the quivers of traditional advertisers. We are talking about the handful that are a good part of the 21st Century Marketing puzzle.

The information below offers the activities—both high level and granular by channel—to demand from your marketing agency partner and/or your in-house sales and marketing team. This is the full package—the full working fiefdom with all the king's horses and men and employees and agencies working to make your kingdom more money, more efficiently.

Some are new-school digital. Some are old-school sales and marketing.

All of them work and when deployed together, make one hell of a solid, scalable, tied-to-net-new-customer-generation long-term playbook.

At a high level, these are the components required for successful, scalable customer generation that maximizes volume of customers or leads while minimizing Cost Per Sale:

THESE ARE THE ADVANCED EIGHT TACTICS

1. Advanced non-tradename search engine advertising on Google and Bing
   a. The benefits and risks of non-TN SEM
   b. How to manage these teams and tactics

2. Advanced social media advertising via Facebook/Instagram
   a. Lookalike+
   b. Rich Media Ads Always
   c. How to manage these teams and tactics

3. Advanced display advertising using a DSP: Demographic and Psychographic "up-funnel" Programmatic

4. Automated telephony marketing: voice and text
   a. Text messaging (primarily for B2C)
   b. Automated Voicemail (for B2C or B2B)

5. Do Direct Mail Right

6. Advanced Lead Nurturing
   a. You must use drastically different creative and messaging and calls to action (and therefore must think where you want these people to go if they click) than the creative that was used to make the lead or customer in the first place.
   b. In controlled experiments with a 45,000-sample set, we

have seen improvements from lead to sale of 60 percent in High Value B2C clients when this type of nurturing is done correctly.

    c.   It is irrelevant whether you think Facebook "works" for your industry or "you don't use Facebook so therefore it doesn't work," this tactic works and works incredibly well while deploying very few media dollars across ALL social media channels, not just LinkedIn. I would strongly argue, based on real data and empirical evidence, that Facebook is still the reigning champion in the ROI battle in both B2B and High Value B2C in the direct response customer generation world.

7.   Do Email Correctly

8.   Cost Per Sale Reporting and Data Pass

    a.   You know what GTM stands for (don't worry . . . to be reviewed below) and it's set up correctly on every page of your website. It's like the reporting and data version of making sure you wear pants and deodorant to work . . . it's beyond essential to do anything.

    b.   Make sure that every lead is followed up from a sales standpoint.

    c.   Your CRM system needs to report on salesperson activity.

    d.   Any speed to lead not measured in minutes or hours is failing.

    e.   Direct mail and/or personal efforts are a must for every lead, and those efforts and outcomes must be tracked.

YOUR COMPANY'S HIGH LEVEL, OMNI-CHANNEL MARKETING VIEW

This is what your future marketing funnel should look like for net new customer generation after the basics (listed above) are taken care of. Viewed as a horizontal journey, the new consumer experience can be imagined with the following stages and tactics, ideally supplemented with high quality call centers and customer nurturing efforts (as seen below):

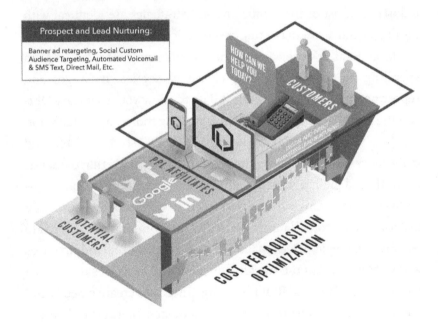

There is no singular marketing battle plan that is perfect for every vertical across B2B and High Value B2C, which is to say that the six out of eight of the puzzle pieces could work for a new VC funded Silicon Valley SaaS company to build their sales pipeline, but the recipe that works for a 110-year-old manufacturing company in Pittsburgh may use only three out of the eight pieces.

Moreover, it's not just about digital marketing. There are many pieces of traditional, offline advertising and marketing that are effective elements in a robust, full stack customer journey. This is about reviewing the whole portfolio of tactics and ad platforms under the 21st Century Customer Generation umbrella and deciding what's right for your company based on your details.

In another playbook, we will review the marketing strategy differences among unique verticals—such as how the world of higher education differs in marketing from that of insurance or B2B manufacturing. But at the core of most B2B and High Value B2C industries, most of the campaigns and strategies are identical with the digital and direct marketing best practice tactics and ad platforms.

In general, it's the same game goal: Getting more efficient in spending money, testing new channels, tactics, messages and reporting intelligently using CRM data to show you what the ROI is (via the Cost Per Acquisition) what's making money and what's not.

Take it from a digital marketing native: Full stack, scalable, and truly successful customer generation focused marketing demands more than digital. You need All Digital + Traditional Channels + Cohesive Messaging . . . and you need to do it in a synchronized fashion (e.g.., proper launch dates that are coordinated). There are essential strategic pieces that need to be present on landing pages and websites and in the tracking of clicks and tying this data into a backend CRM for real ROI reporting. There are creative needs and baseline tactics that work across every industry. There are offline and traditional marketing elements that have a home in 21st Century best practice direct response marketing!

Let's get to all of the scalable best practices for customer generation, beyond the Core Four.

DETAILS OF THE A-8

1. *It is very important to note that for many companies, CEOs, and executives, the following information and detailed tactics are far beyond their level of marketing expertise.*

2. *These notes are only for said CEOs and executives who wish to either (a) self-educate to a more 21st Century Marketing Ninja level, or (b) use this to help them manage their marketing teams and agencies by listing the tactics and to-do list for the people who are actually doing the work.*

3. *The level of granularity in this Chapter is appropriate, in my opinion, for a real AVP-VP-SVP or maybe exceptional CMO to understand. If someone with a job title at this level understands and can speak eloquently about the tactics below, rather than just managing people who understand it, that someone is one hell of a great marketing executive.*

1—ADVANCED SEARCH ENGINE ADVERTISING

An agency's SEM efforts must be perfect—there is no excuse not to use every best-practice ad extension (sitelinks, reviews, 800 numbers, dynamic insertion, as examples) and advanced CPE/CPA analysis at the ad group and keyword level. Below are the campaign details and strategic notes for SEM beyond the Core Four tactic of Tradename Search.

Tactical Must Haves: Your team must ensure the following on Google, Bing and Yahoo:

NON-TRADENAME SEARCH ENGINE MARKETING ("NTN SEM"):

- At a high level, NTN SEM is where you're bidding on keywords crucially relevant to your product, goods, or services that don't use your company's name.
- To scale SEM, often one of best ROI + Volume channel in your marketing customer generation portfolio is Non-Tradename SEM
- I'm not going to go into a lot of detail about what differentiates this from TN SEM because this Chapter is for the more advanced digital and direct marketing tactics. If you're already not familiar with that, you're going to need an agency to handle it ASAP.
- Tradename SEM (TN SEM) is easy to set up and manage. NTN SEM campaigns can get massive—there are possibly hundreds of thousands of keywords, and thousands of ad groups . . .

and some companies spend tens of millions of dollars in this channel alone each month.

- If you don't have at least one or two full time employees with 3-5+ years each in not just NTN SEM media buying, but also the very difficult work of tagging websites, understanding UTM parameters and Google Tag Manager, you're running the risk of writing checks your talent pool can't cash.
- Every day I see companies who "don't think SEM works" because their teams bungled NTN SEM media buys, and basically set fire to money and didn't track/report on things correctly, and blamed it on Google, Bing or Yahoo.

As Coolio said: "If you can't take the heat, get your ass out the kitchen—We on a mission."

SEM MANAGEMENT MUST-DO'S

- Make regular changes to bids and budgets.
- Ensure ad copy is regularly managed or changed according to test results.
- Ensure long-tail keywords are being added through search term reports.
- Ensure irrelevant keywords being negated through search term reports.
- Ensure regular management of display site placements (adding negative placements and other bid adjustments according to performance).

SEM OPTIMIZATIONS MUST-HAVES

- RLSA is magic. Use it. It stands for "remarketing lists for search ads" and if your team doesn't know what this is, it's a good bet that your marketing team isn't very good at advanced paid search engine marketing. The simple version is that RLSA is a moderately advanced way to bid on general keywords you'd never otherwise bid on (e.g.: "open clothes store" or "business education") but you might if they just visited your custom dress shop website yesterday, or were on your MBA page of your small college. (More on this later in this section.)

- Ensure ad groups are monitored and turned off for poor overall ad group performance. This helps to not artificially limit successful keywords within the ad group that is being adversely affected by worse-performing keywords.

- Only pause ad groups that are entirely ineffective—test and learn and optimize if there is long-term potential for good CPE, especially at the service/product level.

- Re-test in the short term and quarterly your under-performing ad groups, and make optimizations at the keyword level within these to allow successful keywords to continue while eliminating poor-performing keywords.

- Clean up duplicate keywords to ensure agency/client not competing against itself in auctions.

- Ensure there are not duplicates within campaigns targeting different geo-regions. Duplicate keywords in different campaigns that have the same geo regions, at the same time of day and day of week, should be reduced to the best-performing effort to avoid self-competition and unnecessarily increase costs per click.

- Enact device-level bid adjustments, including desktop, tablet, and mobile, to be created based on campaign-specific performance.

- Add a negative/vulgar keyword list to ensure negative searchers surrounding Client tradename are not wasting ad spend with their clicks, and Display efforts are not serving to inappropriate or otherwise negative websites.

- Ensure all enabled keywords are at least appearing on the first page of search results.

- Create automated rules to manage campaign- and keyword-specific rules for performance situations where making a change would be universally understood—such as setting a rule to pause a keyword that spends 4 times your Cost per Conversion goal in a month, and gets no conversion activity from it.
- Create rules to ensure keywords are always present on the first page of search results, or paused if ROI potential isn't there due to high cost of competition.
- Create geographic targeting bid adjustments. This can be specific to region, state, or city, depending on accuracy and amount of data available.
- Ensure all keywords are specific to Client products, with high intent to convert, and are not simply indicative of information gathering at a high-funnel level. Such keywords will perform poorly in click-through rates ("CTRs"), conversion rates, and quality score, weighing the entire account down.

STRUCTURE OF SEM MUST-HAVES

- Create keyword match-type specific campaigns (exact, phrase, modified-broad):
  ○ Splitting keyword match-types into their own sister campaigns allows for better monitoring of budget and performance at the campaign level.
  ○ Allow the use of cascading negative keywords (a list of exact-match and phrase-match keywords being bid upon, applied to their more broad-match type counterpart campaigns).
  ○ Enacting this structure has shown an improvement in cost per conversion by anywhere from 12-20 percent for Level Agency clients.

SEM CALL EXTENSIONS MUST-HAVES

- Add call extensions, using campaign-level call tracking, to serve during business hours.
- Make these 800 numbers *unique*—certainly not the ones you use for your homepage on your website. Companies like Twilio offer a great, easy-to-use platform for $1 per month where you can spin up unique 800 numbers. Use this, and ideally use a unique number for every ad group and/or even keyword, if it gets enough clicks.

SEM AD COPY MUST-HAVES

- Ensure all active Search ad groups have Expanded Text Ads (ETAs) enabled.
- Analyze and regularly test current ad copy.
- Create ad iterations that use an ad group's keywords within at least the first two headlines of Expanded Text Ads.
- Ensure that ad group keywords are featured in a logical, human-speech way within the headlines of the ads.
- Make your calls to action compelling, specific, and accurate regarding what the user can expect within the landing page they'll visit.
- Comply with the advertiser's text ad policies.

STRATEGIC MUST-HAVES

ABT: Always Be Testing

Live every day with an "Always Be Testing" approach to media buying in general and paid search engine marketing in particular. No other ad channel is likely as important, unless you're in an industry or company where you built a new mousetrap and no one is searching for your products or services (see Google Search for "iPhone" pre-June 2007) and without question, no digital ad channel is as over-fished as paid search. Even my mom has a Google Ad account; well, not really, but nearly twenty years after the launch of AdWords, you better bet that the only way to scale and win in SEM is to obsess over perpetual CPA and ROI monitoring, and eternal testing.

Test each new copy or call to action idea against previous champion ideas, collect relevant data for those ideas, and determine the winner. At all points in the media funnel, the audience should be tested 100 percent of the time.

Ad Copy tests should run in every enabled ad group in a similar way to how Landing Page tests should run randomized for every visitor (click). User behavior data should be collected, analyzed, reported on, and decisions should be made based on the most successful, statistically-significant result that drives the best return on investment for your company.

CAMPAIGN ORGANIZATION

At a high level, campaigns need to be properly organized by budget item, theme, and keyword match type. Keywords within follow this keyword match type appropriately. Brand efforts are intended to be segregated from non-brand efforts and your campaign appears properly linked to Google Analytics, which can solve for many tracking issues found within the account.

ON MATCH-TYPE SEGMENTATION

There are several reasons to structure the account by creating sister campaigns that separate match types, including:

- You will have better control of budgets by using more relevant keywords (exact) rather than more broadly-reaching terms (broad)
- Higher level understanding of longer-tail, highly-tailored terms (exact-match) and their performance against "wider-net" efforts (broad)
- Reduction of redundancies within one's own account.

At our agency, we recommend accounts be structured in the following way:

- Campaigns are separated by Brand vs. Non-Brand.
- Campaigns are separated by keyword match-types.
- Cascading negative keywords of exact-match terms are applied to more general efforts: phrase, modified-broad, broad.

When cascading negatives are *not* applied, the following will occur in the account:

- Exact-match terms will compete with broad-match terms in different campaigns, driving up costs per click.
- Management of exact-match terms may be inadvertently overridden by sister phrase or broad efforts.
  - For instance, if an exact-match term is paused due to poor performance, instead of ceasing to impress on that term in the account, the broad-match version of that keyword will now impress for that search at a higher cost per click than the exact-match iteration—hurting the optimization effort.

Again, my agency would recommend creating a cascading negative keyword list of exact-match terms within the account, and applying those terms to more general match-type campaigns.

BRAND VS. NON-BRAND SEGMENTATION

Campaigns must be titled to separate brand efforts from non-brand efforts. Don't intermix them—both in terms of how SEM campaigns are build and how you budget for them!

Brand budgets are dedicated 100 percent to brand efforts, while non-brand budgets are similarly dedicated 100 percent to non-brand efforts. This will give media managers more accurate insight and control over budgets and their impacts on brand and non-brand efforts.

And while not always true, especially if there are errors in TN SEM, you typically want to spend as much money as you can on your TN SEM campaigns. Literally, an open checkbook. Bifurcating budgets will help you manage this internally.

RLSA AUDIENCES

RLSA (Remarketing for Search Ads) are a great way to improve ad rank based on whether a searcher has visited your company's web properties or not. Beyond that, media managers may segment these relevant audience members by section of a website—for instance, a list can be built for users who have visited a product or service page, even if they have not filled out a request for information form.

These users are often more likely to engage with ads and landing pages, as we know they are familiar with your brand. Often, if targeted properly, a digital marketer can bid on highly competitive terms, but restrict those bids to just those who are already aware of your company brand –the volume will be much smaller than the general population, but much more highly motivated to engage with your ads and landing pages.

RLSA campaigns must be set up to be "target and bid." If you do not do this, the same keywords that are in these RLSA campaigns and other campaigns are competing against one another, artificially inflating your costs per click.

You will also need your team to change the audience criteria for these groups to cover as many pages on your website as possible if you have multiple websites or properties, thereby providing more audience members for the intended segments.

RLSA bid adjustments in Google and Bing can be an effective tool for improving campaign performance—but only if they are implemented properly at the optimal level of granularity that audience membership can support.

AD SCHEDULES (CALLED "DAYPARTING")

Not only does the volume of people searching for keywords you've bid on and the volume of clicks you get to your landing pages change throughout the day, but the quality of those visitors can change as well. Think about the likely difference in humans who are Googling at 9:01 am versus 2:01 am. That doesn't mean that the person searching in the wee hours is a bad customer. In fact, depending on the type of product or service you offer, that person may be a better customer. I recommend making time of day and day of week bid adjustments based on historic performance, determined by each individual campaign's performance within the account.

Understand your customer and your products. Make some educated guesses as to how to set up your dayparting, run some tests, and see what your CPL and CPA outcomes are. Optimize accordingly.

DEVICE BID ADJUSTMENTS

Your team must optimize device bid adjustments based on campaign-level device performance, increasing bids where conversion volume is high and costs per conversion are low. Similarly, lower bids when conversion volume is low and costs per conversion is high. This should extend beyond just mobile devices, to computers and tablet devices.

TRACKING TEMPLATE

Make sure your team is implementing tracking templates at the campaign level for every campaign. This will have significant benefits to the account, including:

- There will be more consistent use of URL parameters within the account.
- There is a significantly lowered chance for human error in tracking by turning thousands of individual tracking points to dozens or maybe a few hundred.
- Tracking parameter changes will no longer require new ads to be created, which would restart the Google ad review process and take up valuable time to complete (up to 48 hours), during which time ads may be limited or stop impressing entirely.

UTM PARAMETERS

UTM parameters are the pieces of data that look like garbled nonsense in the website address after someone clicks on an ad that tells your marketing world—your Google Analytics account, your CRM and database/data warehouse feeds—more about where a person came from, the word they Googled to find/click on your ad, etc. This is a massive amount of essential information. These need to be used in a way that is compatible with standards used in Google Analytics and/ or are compatible with (meaning the info is consumed correctly and stored) the analytics and CRM/BI Tool/Database your company uses.

We could talk for ten pages about this, but it's important to have a conversation with your media team and agency about making sure the query string parameters are getting passed correctly through from the search engine into the right database.

SERVER-SIDE TRACKING AND CAMPAIGN MANAGEMENT

We recommend deploying click tracking through Google Campaign Manager (FKA DoubleClick), or through a directly-controlled platform, such as Campaign Manager, which allows flexible, prompt execution of management tasks that aren't filtered down by a third-party system.

Keep in mind that this is an advanced step that only some of my clients use—but it allows them to see that prospecting display has a 3 times higher lead volume, and 10 times higher sale volume, than if we only looked at it from a direct spend-to-lead window. So this is important, but only if your team is truly engaged with a good weapons-grade digital agency.

Said another way, if your company is not using a multi-channel attribution funnel (you should) or you aren't planning to in the mid-term, then I wouldn't employ this because it takes a lot of time and leaves a lot of room for human error. Worse still, this will not be up and running quickly, and a novice trying to execute using this system will surely make mistakes that can lead to ads pointing to the wrong landing page, or inadvertently creating broken links.

WEBSITE PHONE CALL TRACKING

Call tracking must be activated so that if a customer were to click on an ad and call your company using the phone number on the website, paid advertising efforts would get proper credit for that phone call. Use a dynamic phone tracking system on the website to properly track phone calls (and resulting conversions/sales) that are generated through paid advertising efforts.

MATCH TYPES

There are three types of ways to target the words someone Googles: broad, phrase, and exact-match keyword targeting.

Broad means that for *any* word in a phrase that a person Googles—truly any other words or phrases in the world—if your keyword or phrase is *in* that mess, and you have broad-matched that word or phrase, your ad could appear.

For example: You work for an online school, a BMW dealer, an IT service company, or Bank of America, and you bid on the phrase "online education" or "local BMW dealer" or "IT services" or "Bank of America." When someone Googles the following things, your ad could appear:

- "What is wrong with education online"
- "local ice cream"
- "IT the movie"
- "list of American banks"

To make matters even more crazy, broad-match keywords are categorical, too. This means that ads may show on searches that include misspellings, synonyms, and other iterations relevant to the search as defined by Google. As an example, bidding on formal shoes will have ads impress for users who search for black wingtips.

You can see how disastrous everything listed above can and will be.

Phrase match means that exact phrase must appear, but can be in any order.

Exact match means literally only that word or phrase can appear to trigger your ad to show.

We recommend reducing the match-types of keywords to exact-match, phrase, and modified-broad only—removing broad-match terms.

Doing so will grant the account:

• More control over potential search query ad impressions.
• More efficient ad impressions at a lower overall cost.
• Less time managing fewer match types across the account.

I don't invest in broad-match terms because of how expensive and unpredictable the impressions may be in this category. Instead, I recommend using modified broad terms, which behave similarly but do not include synonyms or other iterations of the ads. The keywords indicated within the term must appear, in some order (or common misspelling), within the user's search query.

This ensures more control in a more general bidding effort.

FIRST-PAGE BID ADJUSTMENTS

For the love of all that is holy, IT IS NOT ALWAYS NECESSARY—NOR EVEN GOOD—TO BE THE FIRST POSITION IN SEM. I wanted to say that in all caps because it is mind-blowing that in 2020 many people who work in digital marketing still think this is a "thing." It's not a thing. And if it's a thing, it's a bad thing.

However, and in general, Google and I both recommend ensuring any keywords being bid upon should be ranked in, at minimum, the first page of results, but generally in the top of page results.

If you have keywords that are rarely impressing due to having a bid below the first page minimum, this is often a difference of very little from current bids:

There are two avenues to improve ad position across the board:

- Improve quality score.
- Improve keyword bids.

We recommend doing both—starting with increasing bids on any keywords below the first page bid that will require minimal changes, and then focusing on working to improve quality score of those more expensive terms through more relevant, keyword-heavy ad copy and landing pages.

For those that are prohibitively expensive, consider revisiting the strategic inclusion of those terms and remove those unnecessary, irrelevant terms.

Only about 7 percent of users will click on ads after the first page. So the issue is managing key words that are barely providing the juice worth the management and optimization squeeze, so to speak.

2—ADVANCED FACEBOOK AND INSTAGRAM ADVERTISING

One of the biggest wins for marketing professionals who are in the business of customer generation since around 2012 was using the absolutely incredible targeting available on Facebook and, via the same back end platform, Instagram, to put the right ad in front of the right person for an surprisingly reasonable price. Additionally, that advertisement took up the whole damn cell phone screen with amazing rich media and product/service layout options.

In the early days when FB got their act together (meaning their ad targeting, creative options, and cost to advertisers), it was like the early days of mixed martial arts where you had 1000 thug street brawlers against one dude who knew Ninja-level Bruce Lee stuff and Brazilian Jiu jitsu, and that one dude beat everyone. So FB was basically like guys from Brazil with the last name of Gracie.

That was digital marketing on Facebook in 2012-2015 for pretty much everyone who knew how to use Facebook. I'm not going to rehash the general principles of this social media platform (see Chapter 1) or the low-hanging fruit of CAT (see Chapter 3, Core Four tactic #2), but you're going to need to upgrade your social media game on Facebook if you are in a B2B or High Value B2C industry.

If you skipped ahead, run a B2B company, and think "Facebook isn't for business, and what about LinkedIn?" then stop reading and go back and read Chapter 1.

WHAT EXISTS BEYOND FACEBOOK AND INSTAGRAM CAT?

The reality is that, as mentioned before, even though FB/Instagram CAT campaigns are borderline magic and second only to Tradename

SEM in representing the very lowest hanging fruit on the abundant and Avitar-esque-Tree-of-Life in digital advertising, it's still not that scalable.

CAT—again which stands for Custom Audience Targeting—uses your current lead or customer list/database to turn information you already have and turn that into new, repeat, or higher value customers. This is one-to-one targeting using only the email addresses of these records. It's particularly effective but, again, it's limited to how many records you have in your CRM.

But what about reaching people who have never seen your website, brand, product and who have in no way interacted yet with your company?

Sure, you can buy an email list from one of the gazillion database sales companies (infoUSA is one of the more popular) and use that list to power a Facebook or Instagram CAT campaign, but these days they charge extra for you to use their data in this way—even if you already bought the data and have the email addresses to send email campaigns! That to me is complete b.s., and, by the way, a purely fictitious value-add . . . though it's impressive how the search for profit tends to remove common sense in product offerings in a mature product like data sales.

Anyway, you need to use social media to find customers who don't know about you. You need to go upstream. In the life cycle of a consumer, this is all about finding the right customers the day, week, or month before they know enough to Google your company name or hard-key your URL into their browser.

Specifically, this next level for social media advertising for effective and efficient customer is what can be called "prospecting" or "up-funnel" digital marketing. These tactics use the beating heart of what is powerful about these channels. They are what makes Facebook have a $400,000,000,000+ market cap: namely, the targeting based on the demographic and psychographic data points these ad channels have with every user in their system.

We use these data points—things well beyond age, race, location and gender—and dive deep into what users like to buy, their net worth and income, what type of home they own, with whom they live in it, political and hobby-based interests, and dozens and dozens of other real data points taken from or based on each person's profile. Then we take this X-Acto knife of targeting and truly deploy the ultimate battle formation of digital marketing: Put the right ad in front of the right person at the exact right time for a very good price (on typically a cost-per-click basis).

Only on social media can we *really* do this. Search engines do a great job, but they can only know what a human Googles and says what they are interested in searching for—and what you'll advertise at them with. In social media, you *actually know* exactly *who* the person is, at least in terms of things nearly as sensitive as their SSN. Where they work. Their job title. Their income.

That's ultimate advertising power.

Here is how you wield it to scale, beyond CAT campaigns.

ADVANCED FACEBOOK/INSTAGRAM TACTIC #1: LOOKALIKE + ADDITIONAL AUDIENCE FILTERS

Lookalike campaigns are similar to CAT campaigns, but offer a wider reach. In and of themselves, they are too broad, but with a bit of extra tinkering and filtering and narrowing down of one's audience, you can get to a small target pool of humans.

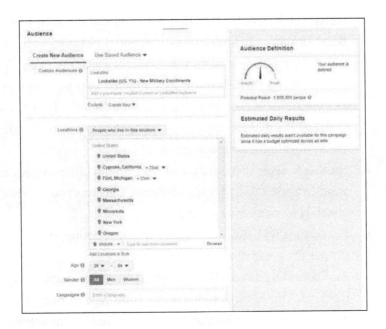

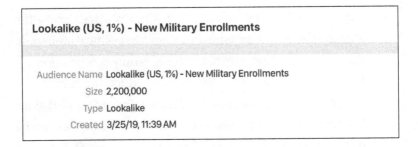

The baseline Lookalike campaign takes an existing client list from your company's database and matches those really important humans to your products/services and gives you 1,000,000 => 10,000,000 new humans "just like them." I've put that last part in quotes because this matching logic is hidden from public view—you don't know how Facebook takes your client list of 2,854 or whatever people and tells you there are a million others who are kindred spirits.

So at a high level, here are some notes:

- It's more effective for B2C than B2B, but still a worthy test in B2B as long as you filter and narrow your Lookalike audience down. In a B2C world, it's OK to target 100,000+ people in each ad set but in B2B, for most companies, keeping it to low five figures or even south of 10,000 individuals helps reduce impressions that are wasted by being shown to people who are irrelevant for your company.

- Facebook deploys its matrix of data points of customers in your list against its own wider audience and gives you matches, which is by no means perfect.

- But starting with this as a baseline targeting option, then going deeper is a great campaign to test.

- Additional targeting options should be more than demographic markers. The point is to keep the same type of people and get more relevant with them, not just to reduce the number of people.

- Some examples of targeting options—filters—that narrow the audience by customer type are things like political affiliation, gender, income/net worth, interests, family composition.

- Examples of targeting options that reduce the number of targets or focuses your sales and messaging tactics are things like location and age. While people from Wisconsin can be different from people from Georgia, that type of filter and targeting options really aren't the best ways to narrow the audience. But they are great ways for companies to get smarter with messaging, or point people to the correct store location or sell warm weather clothes vs. cold weather clothes.

So, use Lookalikes plus additional targeting filters to build social media campaigns that target entirely new consumers for your company.

ADVANCED FACEBOOK/INSTAGRAM TACTIC #2:
Rich Media Driven Ad Units

It's borderline inconceivable how many amazing ways to visually advertise to people there are in Facebook and Instagram, and how much this one company pushed the advertising world to fully using the power of smartphones.

This story is similar to how the iPhone allowed people to understand how terrible the Treo, Blackberry and Palm Pilot "smart" phones were to access websites built after 1999. The iPhone's advantage completely embarrassed the competition, and changed what was thought possible from a handheld device. Facebook and Instagram have completely defined and are still the bedrock definition of immersive audio-visual advertising online. Banner ads? Twitter? Any other social network, even giants like LinkedIn? As of 2020, every single way for an advertiser to visually and audibly communicate with a target demographic still sucks in comparison with Facebook and Instagram.

This single reality is one of the most powerful and under-appreciated facts you need to grasp in B2B and B2C direct response customer generation advertising. Yes, I said B2B. If you don't know what I'm talking about and think that "Facebook isn't for business, but LinkedIn is," you need to stop reading immediately and go back to Chapter 1 because you're going to set fire to a ton of money if you don't.

Unless you sell paper towels or something that requires no explanation or has no point of differentiation (your product or service is identical to everything else in the market), you need to convey to a prospective customer the following things:

1. What your thing is.
2. Why they need your thing.
3. Why your company is the best option to go to for this thing.

Consider the customer journey (above from Chapter 1) from complete unawareness that they need anything and never heard of your company to the point of sale where they become a faithful new customer in your CRM:

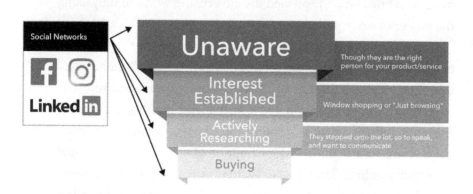

The beauty, again, is not just the finely tuned targeting of your prospective customers based on dozens of demographic and psychographic points that laser in on why they are a good target all the way from 100 percent Unaware => Interested but just browsing => Actively shopping. The beauty is also the pricing—typically, a crazy-fair shared risk model of Pay Per Click where the ad platform shows your ad for free until someone does something you like . . . like click on your ad and head toward your website. As I said before, a real weapons-grade, Tier 1 digital agency will buy most of their media on a CPM basis and back into a CPC goal . . . but that's splitting hairs. For the lion's share of readers of this book, the CPC precept is gold.

But it's also the fact that a good ad on Facebook can do the following things that, again, amazingly as of 2020, no other ad platform lets you do as well:

1. Takes up the entire screen of your cell phone with an ad. Seriously. Just check your Facebook feed.
2. Uses video and animated, or static images that can change.

3. Uses audio, obviously. And while 90 percent of people don't listen to the audio on Facebook videos, they *do* read the subtitles . . . which requires that you develop audio.
4. Provides a user experience where you can often show a robust list of products, certainly for those of you who run companies selling physical products, and it can mimic to an incredible degree of amazingness your eCommerce site or product page.

Simply, the ad units that Facebook offers your marketing team to use should be like watching my kids in an unlocked and unguarded candy store. With kittens and Golden Retriever puppies. And all those new British kids' cartoons.

Here are seven ad units you need to test—as long as they are appropriate for your product or service line. At minimum, you should be running three of them, even for the most traditional B2C/B2B or service B2B company.

- Single video ad unit—Take those awesome explainer videos or client testimonials or 30-60-90 spots telling why your company is amazing and deploy them in a direct response ad.
- Single image ad unit—The most basic ad unit, but again it captures nearly the entire screen on most cell phones and is the baseline for direct response up-funnel advertising.
- Collection ad unit—an amazingly faithful recreation of your eCommerce site or product-heavy non-eCommerce site.
- Carousel ad unit—up to ten images scrolling horizontally that showcase a range of your products or, if you are a service business, the different industries you serve or solutions you provide.
- Slideshow—this uses static images vs. video, but employs sound and motion.
- Instant Experience (formerly called Facebook Canvas ads)—

the Rolls Royce treatment more for brand advertising, or appropriate for rolling out a new product or a re-branding of your company. Big announcement-type stuff.

- Lead Generation Ads (called "Lead Ads")—You use either the image, video, or carousel ad units above and, instead of being driven to your company's website/landing pages, you immediately are driven to a simple Facebook page with the prospective customer's information *already populated* into a lead gen form (because FB already knows your name, phone number and email). All the prospect needs to do is click the button—and you've got a lead. This is an amazing method to shortcut the user experience in lead generation: higher volume, lower qualification vs. driving someone to your landing page, but for some B2B service verticals and specific B2C products, this is the best way to *start* the sales conversation.

The bottom line is that you must ideally deploy ads with rich media/video and a reason why your company and product service line needs to be listened to immediately. Lazily using static images and boring copy is going to set your money on fire.

Act like Facebook is the most powerful weapon marketers have been given in nearly twenty years, pound out some fresh video or recycle some killer video testimonials of your current clients and customers, and test some of these ad units listed above.

And I'm begging you to not fall into the trap where, because your company isn't in Cali with employees named Zola, Thaaad (where the "d" is silent) or "Lennyn with 3 n's and all the y's are o's" with bullshit job titles like Chief Happiness Officer, Senior Growth Evangelist, or _____ (any word here)-in-Residence, you're afraid that this is not for your company.

It is.

100 percent.

Your company. It's for any company selling tires or yachts or SaaS solutions or heavy equipment leases and dump bodies or spatulas or financial advising services or checking accounts or educations—any company that needs new clients beyond the ones who search for products on Google.

Advance paid advertising on Facebook and Instagram, not merely putting content on your company's page to talk to people who already know you, can be profitable for every company **if done right.** Every company includes old-school B2B that your granddaddy started in Akron, Ohio, new-school B2B that has eight figures of VC capital and a twelve-month sales cycle, and B2C anything at all.

Trust me. Data doesn't lie, and wielding the most surgical digital advertising weapon bears fruit for your sales pipeline.

TACTICAL EXECUTION IN MANAGING ADVANCED SOCIAL MEDIA TEAMS

Standardized Naming Convention

One of the best ways know when the account is structured properly is when anyone in the organization could spend five minutes looking at the account overview and get a good grasp of what they are looking at. Being able to accomplish this depends heavily on being highly organized and sticking to a specific naming convention that gives information such as objective goal, audience, placement, geo, and age. This will allow you to read and understand reports at a glance— thereby allowing you to make bidding and budgeting decisions quickly, efficiently, and with confidence.

Budget and Schedule

When it comes to budgeting, you have the choice between Daily and Lifetime budgets. The clear majority of Ad Sets are set to Daily budgets. In conversations with Facebook and in my own experience, it has been recommended as of 2020 to run with Daily budgets as opposed to Lifetime budgets as long as, after a few weeks, you don't change the Daily budget more than about 15 percent each day. But this just changed. In years before, it was Lifetime that was showing the strategic edge. So, this recommendation changes and you need a team or a resource in digital advertising to tell you when the winds of the ad platforms change . . . and they will.

Some details for the nerds of the flock who have read this far (you are my people, btw): Facebook has gotten smart about the Daily budget model and allows itself to spend more or less 20 percent of the Daily budget per day, depending on day of week ("DOW") and success (though on average, over the course of a week/month, it will spend to that Daily budget).

Because this seems to change every six months, I want to highlight the importance of testing the Monthly/Lifetime budget aspect often to see what kind of results you get for your campaigns.

To further explain by way of example, Daily budgets tell Facebook's ad delivery algorithm to spend that budget no matter what—regardless of actual performance. Lifetime budgets allow Facebook's ad delivery algorithm to work as it was intended—to determine over a specified timeframe the optimal deployment of a given budget.

In general, the rule of thumb to determine the number of ad sets you can support is by figuring out your cost-per-conversion and allowing for double your cost-per-conversion for each ad set you have live. For example, if your average cost per lead is $50, then you would want to be able to spend $100 per day per ad set, or about $3,000 per ad set per month. If your monthly budget is $200,000, then you could support a total of sixty-six ads sets at a maximum.

Target Audiences

Overlapping audiences causes an increase in the bid you need to pay to win the auction to have Facebook serve your impression, and because you are competing against yourself, you will eventually start to see a decrease in impression volume within the different ad sets as they fight to serve impressions to the same audience. So, make sure you don't have a ton of audience overlap across campaigns.

Age Targeting

Do *not* have extremely broad age targeting. This is exceedingly bad for ROI and ostensibly negates the power that Facebook targeting can provide.

For example, if Ad Sets are set to either 14–65+ or 18–65+, you are eliminating one of the easiest ways to put the right ad in front of the right customer. Why? Because if you treat an 18-year-old the way you treat a 65-year-old, even with the *exact* same psychographic profiles and markers, you are missing a massive and simple targeting opportunity. And better, more narrow targeting typically allows you to be more effective and efficient with your advertising efforts.

Instead, separate age groups into different Ad Sets so that the ad copy and ad itself can speak directly to the appropriate prospective audience. This will allow you to view results more granularly to determine which ad set is generating the most leads at the best cost per lead, giving you the data you need to move budget to where it will do the most work for you.

3—ADVANCED DISPLAY ADVERTISING

If you think that it's a good idea—or even an okay idea—to buy banner ads through your local or regional newspaper's website, or your industry's trade magazine, for the love of all the gods in all the heavens and teas in China: STOP.

I'm serious. Stop everything you are doing and listen, because these are the four greatest truths you need to hear to take your marketing out of the Bronze Age and save yourself from the shame of quietly setting your marketing budgets on fire.

TRUTH #1: Buying banner ads on individual websites is quite possibly the greatest waste of money in the digital space, and the greatest hallmark of bad digital marketing since Pets.com spent 22.7 percent of their booked Q1 FY2000 revenue on a 30-second Super Bowl commercial (hint: Don't do that! Yes, there was a spike in traffic but their P&L couldn't handle it).

TRUTH #2: If anyone in your marketing team or at your "agency" (those quotes are there on purpose) tells you that it's a good idea, you need to seriously reconsider their role as a marketer. I'm not saying you should fire them. Heck, maybe Jimmy or Suzie would be a darn good receptionist, but they are a bad digital marketer in 2020.

TRUTH #3: You need to buy banner ad impressions like you buy every other impression on search engines and social networks: with a borderline 100 percent definitive understanding of what kind of person every impression belongs to. Crossing your fingers does not work.

TRUTH #4: Buying banner ads on a single website is the digital version of buying a billboard on I-95. You have no idea whose eyeballs are driving by.

So let's get to the fancy talk, shall we?

TYPES OF CUSTOMER TARGETING AND WHY A DSP IS IMPORTANT

Banner ad retargeting—the act of creating a cookie pool of every visitor to every Client website (and landing pages)—and the intelligent, targeted, and copy-specific way to advertise only to these individuals is a must-have. Every company must do this. Retargeting display is inexpensive and is the best way to remarket to those who have already shown interest in your company's products and services.

DSP or "Programmatic" display advertising is the use of advanced NASDAQ-like marketplaces where you buy ad impressions and you know who each person is, or at minimum you know the demographic and psychographic persona of each eyeball attached to each impression bought. This is advanced and more complicated than the strategy most agencies and marketing teams use (GDN = Google's Display Network . . . or, as it's called now, Google Ads) to buy ads on specific websites. Programmatic Display Advertising is the future and the CPA efficiencies far outweigh standard display media buying tactics. Simply, it's no longer important where or on what website you got the human being you are targeting, it's important that you know *to whom* you are advertising regardless of where you find them.

PROGRAMMATIC DISPLAY—THE DETAILS

- Agency *must* use Display Video 360 (DV360), the industry's leading DSP platform, the gold standard and most advanced.
- It is a larger network that includes GDN.
- You'll have more targeting options (third-party data).
- It offers better tracking of assisted conversion data.

Keep in mind, per the notes regarding up-funnel social media advertising above, that your company's future battleground for net new customers isn't as much search engines as it is the world your future customers live in *before* they Google something relevant to your company. SEM is still king of good digital ROI and "bottom-funnel" customer generation. And you likely have a ton of work to do before you tap out that channel and hit a point of diminishing returns.

But you've got to get in front of your future clients and customers (a) before they know they need your product, and (b) before your competitors do the same. As I've said before, the reason any agency worth their salt needs to be borderline perfect in SEM is because it's getting fished out for many industries. I've jokingly said my mom has a Google Ads account, and if I wait a few more years, that might actually be true. What is definitely true is that your up-funnel game is where you can beat your competitor to your future clients. SEM is the ecosystem where you've got to bring your A-game or risk falling into obsolescence today. Paid social and display advertising as of 2019 still has room for you to make a play to be a leader in digital customer acquisition in your industry.

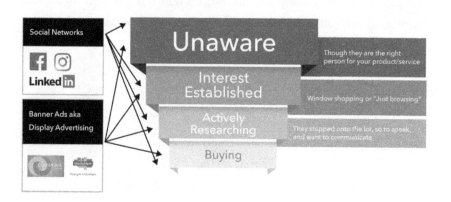

Where BANNER ADS (AKA DISPLAY ADVERTISING) Drive Action:
THROUGHOUT the SALES CYCLE

GOOGLE ADS VS. PROGRAMMATIC DISPLAY— DEPLOYING IT

The good news is that your in-house digital team or an average digital agency can run Google's standard network display adverting pretty darn well using some *good* but not weapons-grade digital targeting and sequencing levers.

Google Ads—the same platform that your team or agency uses for the core search engine ads—has an absolutely massive display network. And before you ask, *yes* . . . there are other display networks out there. *No* . . . I do not think they can deliver on the promise to have better ROI via some magic black box targeting they've come up with. That's dated, late-'90s/early 2000s sales garbage from back when everyone and their uncle had a display ad network with special targeting, blah blah blah. Don't fall for it. If you want to upgrade from basic banner ad retargeting (a C4 tactic), you should just use Google Ads for display. You can do 75 percent of what you *really* need to do and not get taken to the toolshed by some huckster display network company selling you on how they really know how to target your market/customers.

Trust me—it's like renting a car and signing up for their GPS device. Literally no one outside of grandparents should be doing that. And you shouldn't trust a non-Google display network just because they use fancy sales words and promise to target your audience because of their special database/customer profiles. In the hands of in-house marketing teams and most agencies, these Google people can sell ice to Eskimos, and you should direct your teams to use Google's core display network to go up-funnel if you're not using a DSP.

The bad news?

Running display ads in a DSP requires a digital marketing agency that's legit. I mean A-team, fully stacked with math-and-ROI-driven nerds who love obsessing over a complex ad platform and mastering its dozens and hundreds of options for buying the eyeballs that each impression is attached to . . . and knowing that it's more important to know *who* the person is than *where* they see your banner ad.

Ninety-eight out of a hundred marketing agencies and in-house marketing teams cannot do this. That's the flat-out truth. If you're not going to pony up and go with an elite team, don't worry. As I said before, just use Google Ads' display network for up-funnel banner ads beyond just retargeting, and you'll be ahead of most people in your vertical, unless you're in one of the super competitive B2C or eCommerce verticals. Then you better suck it up, put on the gloves, and get into the ring before your competitors have their brands and products and services fully stuck into the minds of your potential customers months before they actively start shopping. Then it's too late or, at best, an uphill battle and higher Cost Per Acquisition to pry them away and onto your doorstep and sales funnel.

4—AUTOMATED TELEPHONY MARKETING: VOICE AND TEXT

Beyond digital marketing, there are traditional marketing tactics which are effective in ROI+ B2B customer generation. After the lead is generated, and primarily for B2C verticals and some B2B where this type of experience would be appropriate, there is nothing more direct and cost effective as a "closing agent" than a phone-based follow-up.

That's literally why you have a sales team, right?

But let's talk about things that have the following magic marketing qualities: Automated, cheap, and effective. And I love things in marketing that have that holy trifecta of awesomeness.

In a perfect world, you know 100 percent that your sales team is doing the following things every day:

- Following up on *every* lead with a call
- Calling that lead *quickly*, within minutes or, at most, within an hour for B2B
- Following up via text or email
- Making sure that email and/or text message does not suck and isn't just an automated piece of boilerplate saying "Thanks for submitting a lead."

But, guess what I've found in working with some of the best sales environments in America? *Very rarely are even half of these things happening.*

Scary, right? If I were you, and I paid salespeople good money to close and the things listed above were as simple as it gets, I would be pissed if those things were not happening. So if you want to scare the hell out of yourself and lose a ton of sleep wondering what other

"100 Percent Definitely Happening" things are 100 percent definitely *not* happening in your organization, then don't take my word for it (though you really should). Instead, submit 10 leads through different places in your marketing channels, and not all in the same place.

As a simple rule of thumb, any speed to lead contact not measured in minutes or hours is failing. And that's just the tactical efficiency of reaching out via phone, plus there's the quality of the call/voicemail, direct response language and what the call to action is, the existence of a good email or text message, and where those try and drive people (hint: it's neither your homepage nor your landing page that made the lead in the first place!).

It's called "secret shopping" and it's the simplest way of finding out what's really happening in your sales funnel. Do the following if you're not going to take my word for it that, probably, your sales team is not doing 50 percent of what they should be doing from the block and tackling aspects of Salesmanship 101.

1. Ask your IT department to spin up ten numbers in Twilio that all call into one new phone number with a voicemail that is *not* your voice (use the default voicemail message). This will take them 30 minutes even if they are drunk and don't know what they are doing, and it'll cost $15 and it's incredibly easy.

2. If you really want to see what's going on, head to Gmail or another platform and spin up ten new email addresses.

3. Go to your main website and submit five leads—one per day—using fake names and these phone numbers and email addresses if you have them.

4. Do the same via any other marketing channel—and by this time after reading this book, you better be running at least Tradename Search Engine Marketing, so that's at least another route to use instead of your main website lead form.

5. See what phone calls you get, and when they called (these reports are the most basic ones available in Twilio and every

other telephony SaaS platform used to spin up new numbers).
6. See what emails you get.
7. See what text messages you receive, if that's appropriate for your industry.

And you're going to have a heart attack. If you don't, then walk down to your VP of Sales and take them to lunch.

But if you find some serious problems with the speed, quality, and regularity of your sales team's follow-up efforts, these automated marketing tactics can help patch some of the holes in your sales funnel. It's not a perfect fix, but it will guarantee that you're not completely dropping the ball on new, precious leads.

Let's talk about two easily deployable tactics that help improve the speed, quality, and regularity of and your sales team's efforts and help your customers move more readily through your sales funnel:

- Automated Ringless Voicemail
- SMS Text—if B2C

Both of these marketing campaigns are self-explanatory, and there are dozens of third party SaaS vendors who offer low-cost, self-service tools for doing this in-house. The details are as follows:

- Automated Voicemail submission allows you to:
  ◦ Put a pre-recorded message into the recipient's voicemail without ringing.
  ◦ Do this ideally 24 hours after the lead receives the direct mail campaign.
  ◦ Give the recipient a unique 800 number to call back or a website and "tiny"/short URL to visit.
- Text Message
  ◦ Sent with no more than 160 characters.
  ◦ SMS is most effective during business hours (10am–

8pm), whereas lifestyle-oriented activities like internet browsing and mobile app use dominate the early morning and late evening hours.

○ Mondays traditionally have the lowest response rates.

○ The worst times of day to send messages are during common rush hours when people can't read or engage with SMS. This is generally between 6:30–8:30am and 4–7pm local time.

○ Knowing this, segment SMS lists by time zone and then send schedule accordingly.

○ Give the recipient a unique 800 number to call back or a website and "tiny"/short URL to visit.

○ As is the case with email campaigns, make sure that you have a website/landing page that is appropriate for who this person is—they are a lead, and have already gone through your main website or product/service landing page! Please build out a landing page that helps drive them through the sales funnel. Give them different information and have a different call to action than what they've already seen via the lead gen process!

Suggested low-cost vendors are as follows . . . but please do your research as there are ton of other options:

• Automated Voicemail: https://straticsnetworks.com/

• SMS Text: https://www.callfire.com/products/text-messaging and http://trumpia.com/

The prices vary from $0.03 to $0.10 per SMS text solution and a similar fee for automated voicemails.

If you view a flow chart of most B2B or High Value B2C sales funnels and customer journeys, see where the test/automated VM can be placed for, again, low cost and helping to, at minimum, improving your team's speed-to-lead which is how quickly to reach out to a prospective customer post-lead creation.

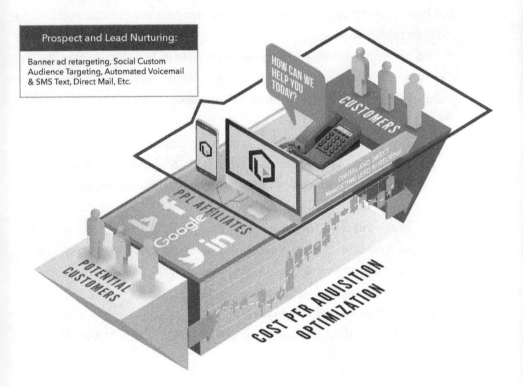

5—DO DIRECT MAIL RIGHT

I'm not going to waste time defining this or talking about a strategy as old as the postal service. If you're already running a DM campaign and have that framework, just make sure that you are *positive* you are doing the following.

Do not lie to yourself—or let your marketers lie by omission. I'm serious. Everyone gets too comfy for the good of the business at some point, especially if they're not the CEO or owner.

1. Be absolutely certain that every six months you are testing new copy, new print cost tiers (e.g., a cheaper or more expensive version), new cadence to mail flights and frequency strategies, and new designs
2. Make this test a low-risk 90-10 test, meaning that 90 percent of your targets get the same old, same old. Only 10 percent get the new test campaign. Track results. See what happens. *Do not stop testing—do this a few times a year!*
3. Rinse, repeat twice per year.
4. When in doubt, *assume absolutely none of this testing is already happening*

The most common thing we find is that the same direct mail strategy is being used for years. One client example saw an amazing company deploying nearly $10,000,000 annually in direct mail where they had been using the same DM package for over five years. Years!

If it ain't broke, it might just be because you didn't pay attention.

If you're not testing, you're failing.

So, that's if your firm already has a DM strategy. But what about if you're not running DM?

Direct mail campaigns starting from scratch should start with a low-cost, low-risk, test-and-learn ethos. These new DM tests need to be produced quickly and with small budgets and should be the combination of the following:

- A current piece of collateral for the product, service, or division in question that might not be the perfectly tailored piece for the module in question, but whose goal is to reassure the legitimacy of the overall company.
- A one-pager describing the benefits of the module printed on, at minimum, 80-lb. text or 65-lb. cover glossy paper (the printer knows what this means), with a digital signature of the business lead for your product line. Keep it simple.

SEGMENTING TO TEST AND LOWER COSTS

You have leads that come in from different channels. And, if you've heeded the prior chapters in this book, every one of them, including the traditional customer generation channels, is tracked so you know the Cost Per Acquisition and ROI.

- From a direct mail standpoint, testing into this tactic should be met with very high standards of who to send an expensive piece to, even if that cost is less than $1 per lead.
- If you are in the B2B world, any decent lead, and especially a qualified sales lead with a decision maker, should get one of these kinds of direct mail:
  - ° Your one-pager laying out your core value proposition— Why Us vs. Them?
  - ° Your by-client/by-industry/by-type, or the "I pay attention to the fact that you're different from other people" piece of collateral. In my world, that's by industry. My company

is B2B, and we work across many different verticals in the B2B and High Value B2C/Luxury Goods space. So I need to talk to those people differently.

This piece that speaks to the exact person can be a letter and not a whiz/bang piece of collateral. This must be focused by industry or by service type, or narrow the audience down in some appropriate way.

But in the B2C world, you've got a *ton* of leads coming in, so if you have not done direct mail before, this is how you should start to lower costs and test into this channel from an ROI standpoint:

✓   TIER 1 *always* gets a direct mail piece.
✓   Any channel that is an outlier of the highest Lead => Sale converting channel
✓   SEO leads
✓   Organic traffic leads
✓   Any channel that gives you leads that might not convert that well, but there is a very important business reason to grow that line/product/segment anyway (e.g., you opened a new physical location, entered a new vertical, have a new suite of services).

CAMPAIGN DETAILS

When you do send a direct mail campaign, use First Class USPS mail and an efficient, nationwide direct mail house with experience in your vertical's work. You want it to be able to report back on a lead level basis (this is very important) the delivery data of each piece. We recommend a firm that a peer of yours currently uses and one you can lean on for a cheap test, promising to increase your budget when it yields results. Then get a competitive second offer just in case! DM is rife with cases of overcharging.

The direct mail campaigns must have the following strategy if you're just getting started:

- Only send once. Leave the multi-tiered DM strategies for later, after you confirm that your customer base responds to a baseline effort.
- Have a direct mail company handle the returned pieces and pay to have the database appended to correct for any failures.
- Have the email, custom digital banner ad/social network, and telephony-based outreach campaigns all ready to execute the day before the First Class deliveries are to arrive.
- While the timing of the direct mail piece is "the sooner the better," the timing of the subsequent strategic digital pieces is essential. Basically, make sure that you don't have the most expensive piece of your tactic (the direct mail piece) arriving ten days before/after you start the text, display ad and social ad CAT one-on-one targeting. Instead, plan for them to occur within 24-48 hours, and keep the digital messages going for a week after the DM piece arrives. I'm not the only one who leaves unopened mail on the counter for days until I get to it.

Quick win, short runway direct mail should not be overthought. Keep it cheap. Make sure you borrow existing collateral to ensure there is *one* gorgeous piece of collateral in the mailer, and back it up with a low-cost one-page piece pointing out the value of your firm, your solution, your service, your uniqueness.

Remember, test DM campaigns often! I cannot overstate how often companies that are doing DM are squandering precious percentage increases in efficiency by failing to test new methods, costs, sending/frequency strategies, copy, and images.

6—ADVANCED LEAD NURTURING

If there is a silver bullet in most High Value B2C verticals and in the B2B space from the standpoint of (a) not many of your competitors are doing this correctly, (b) it's cheap from a dollars-spent-in-media realm, (c) it is automatable and scalable across all of your inbound leads, and finally and most importantly (d) it is *very* profitable, this is it: LEAD + CUSTOMER NURTURING.

Let's break this down into your two worlds from a new business standpoint:

1. You have *old leads* in your database that you paid good money for and worked hard to get. Turn those into *new customers*. A consumer's reality changes with time; the fact they did not turn into a customer from a lead 6-24+ months ago has no bearing on their needs *today*. Monetize old leads.
2. You have *new leads* that just came in within the past 30 days. Super duper. But after the lead is created, is your digital advertising doing *anything* to help your sales team?

If the same channels are the *best*, hands down/empirically proven, at driving new leads on a good Cost Per Acquisition basis, why can't those same digital channels help a lead become a new customer? The answer is—*they can*.

Here is the playbook:

You're going to use the ability of the social networks and DSP banner ad platforms to target humans using their email address. And you have their email address because they are a lead . . . and that's obviously a required field.

So, for literally *every* human you have in your CRM with an email address, you are going to immediately deploy the following tactics. *Yes*, you should segment your social media and display ads to what product/store/service they wanted per their lead information. Tailor your message.

The landing pages? Yes, people are going to click on ads and respond to the subsequent telephony tactics and they need to go somewhere. So send them to a web page/landing page that is not your home page and that is not the same landing page that they saw originally!

Here are the tactics and ad platforms you'll be using and the detailed strategy:

CAMPAIGN DETAILS

✓ **All Aged Leads** => Take ALL of your leads across all digital and direct/offline channels ("Omni-Channel"). Yes. All of them. Why not? You paid for them . . . and they are sitting there.
  ° Definition of "Aged Lead" = After your firm has completed the new inbound lead contact, leads will fall into lower priority and lower touch marketing and call center efforts.
  ° Nurturing efforts will drive to a branded landing page that has a primary and secondary call to action:
    ▪ Primary = "Re-inquire and get to know our company/product again since you may have last heard about us months/years ago."
    ▪ Secondary = "Buy now/Apply now/Inquire now" link if they *do* know you/your product and don't need a bunch of qualifying content.
  ° All landing pages will have a unique 800 number driving calls to a call center as a tertiary call to action, to give people every way to reach out to you, but definitely offer them:

- A unique 800 number for what we call re-inquiries
- A lead gen form that asks them to clarify what they need
- A chat feature if you are shooting for the stars and are great at offering customers every channel to get in touch with your company

° With aged leads, the landing page is heavily messaged to excite and educate on your value proposition, using engaging animated and video-based assets.

° Digital Channels to be used, because you can use the lead's email address as you did in the Core Four Social and Display CAT retargeting world!
  - Social = Facebook and Instagram
  - Display = DSP Email Targeting (via a DSP) and Google Customer Match via email match

° Direct Channels to be used, per the Advanced Eight Telephony Tactics referenced above:
  - Automated voice
  - Text => LP

✓ **All New Leads** => Same Omni-Channel All Leads, digital and direct/traditional

° Definition of "New Lead" = Within 30 days upon launch of the campaign and as each new lead comes into your CRM and is contacted by sales team.

° Nurturing efforts will drive to a branded landing page that has a primary and secondary call to action:
  - Primary = "Apply Now/Buy Now/Sign Up Now/Get Started," etc.
  - Secondary = "Speak with a Sales Representative/ Download info or white paper"

° All landing pages should have unique 800 number driving

calls to a unique call center experience.

- ° Landing page should be heavily messaged to excite and show your firm's consumer outcomes, using animated and video-based assets. You need to give a deep dive into your value proposition at this exact opportunity.
- ° Digital Channels to be used:
  - Social = Facebook and Instagram
  - Display = DSP Email Targeting (via a DSP) and Google (via Google Display Video 360 DSP)
- ° Direct Channels to be used:
  - Automated voice
  - Text => LP
  - Direct mail test for the following lead sources only:
  - Organic;
    - SEM, and possibly Tradename only, instead all of SEM (this should be a business decision based on your budget); Direct mail efforts must remain focused on low cost/high impact

CROSS SELLING

The reality is that after you re-engage your aged lead database and you nurture your new leads, there is still a ton of juice to squeeze from your world of customers. Enter cross selling via digital channels. Consider it current customer nurturing, but in a more sophisticated way than you are currently conducting that tactic.

If you ask my wife, as the joke goes, she'll say I'm wrong about most things and only right about admitting being wrong :-). But at the risk of knowing nothing about your business, I can guess what 95 percent of you do to take your current clients and make them come back for more/to be better, more long-term/high value clients.

Ready?

You email them. A lot.

And I need to tell you that in addition to email being the most over-used and over-relied upon channel, it's just not being smart with all the other digital tools at your disposal.

Yes, emailing your current customers is important. But please, do not let that be the only arrow in your quiver, and please do not mistake a nice way to reach out perhaps every week or every month turn into a giant lever you pull every day/every other day to drum up new revenue.

Email campaigns are so overused that the entire channel is approaching borderline irrelevancy. As part of a cross-selling, omni-channel mix where a current customer in gets an email two or four times a month, it absolutely is effective.

But carpet bombing your customer database with a few emails a week—or daily, which is what I've seen often in the B2C space!!!—is flat-out lazy and destroys email as a channel for your company in the long run.

So let's focus instead on a more advanced media mix that is not rocket science, can be worked to an extent with an in-house team or mediocre agency (though to do well requires a good digital, omni-channel agency), and is going to significantly increase the net present value (NPV for all you CFO's reading this) of each current customer in your database.

CROSS SELLING VIA OMNI-CHANNEL DETAILS

In addition to the significant by-customer-type creative (hint: rich media vs. static ads) and landing page work to be performed (hint: show current clients a site or offer or web page that implies that you know who they are and what they bought/own/use), below is a list of the marketing channels you should use in concert for cross-selling nurturing efforts.

- Your Sales Team/Call Centers
- Email in moderation.
- Facebook/Instagram CAT/Lead level targeting via email address
- Other telephony (automated voicemail, SMS text)
- Google's Customer Match Display via email address
- Rich Media Display retargeting via DSP match
- Direct Mail, possibly only for organic/SEM leads or high value clients/customers . . . which your CRM should be able to tell you very quickly

As we have explained every tactic listed above in prior sections and chapters, I will assume that you're already aware of the power of each item.

As Voltaire said,* we must all cultivate our gardens . . . and your garden has a lot of work that can be done with the green fields already before you.

(*I can hear my sophomore-year Philosophy professor running to her desk to write me a letter changing my grade from a cursed B+ to the A she knew I deserved . . . .)

7—DO EMAIL RIGHT

Email campaigns are likely the most overused form of advertising. The simple fact is that quantity loses to quality and timing. Marketing executives, I've found, have little data-driven understanding about how to craft a quality email, and they often don't take the time and mental bandwidth to think through the right timing strategy. Instead, they solve by carpet bombing inboxes around the world.

Don't do that. Take your time. Don't treat email like an all-you-can-eat buffet in undergrad at 2am. Be surgical and take the time up front to treat each " send" as a different campaign.

The following are parameters for successful email campaigns when looking to engage prospective B2C or B2B contacts and take them from the Lead to Sale. Best practices vary based on industry, prospective client category, or product/service category, but use these tips as a solid starting point.

But most importantly, regardless of your industry:

1.   Build an A-B test.
2.   Run the test and learn.
3.   . . . and make your own best practices.

So here is where to start:

There should be at minimum four emails, well timed to occur no more frequently than seven calendar days apart, and which together tell a story or help a prospective B2C customer or B2B client to understand the value of your offer while at the same time softly overcoming anticipated objections.

In simple terms, the first and last email should be more direct response and forward in terms of the call to action than the middle series.

IMPORTANT STRATEGIES FOR EMAIL #1 AND #4:

- GOAL: To generate a macro-conversion (sale)
- Special promotional offer to drive incremental conversion activity
- Simple headline with clear CTA above the fold
- Clear category delineation for easy browsing
- Condensed format to make content easy to absorb and prevent audience fatigue

IMPORTANT STRATEGIES FOR EMAILS #2 AND #3:

- GOAL: To generate micro-conversion activity by providing value to the recipient
- Friendly, helpful tone
- Messaging designed to provide customer value and generate customer activity
- Generate affinity for the brand doing the sending

EMAIL BEST PRACTICES FOR OVERALL STRATEGY:

- Know your goals.
  - Lead generation-first emails can, and should, be measured differently than Nurturing Emails. Plan, measure and optimize accordingly for each email blast. They have different KPIs.
  - The 1st and 4th email should be measured in terms of traffic to relevant landing pages (NOT your homepage).
  - The 2nd and 3rd emails should be measured in terms of clicks on links within the email to get additional content.

- Be personal.
  - ° Provide content that is relevant and useful.
  - ° Use dynamic content correctly.
    - ✓ Insert first name.
    - ✓ Have different content based on the area of the country, and the product line inquired about.

- Subject lines:
  - ° Short, customized and interesting
  - ° Goal is to pique interest and get an open.

- Go for small wins.
  - ° It's not always about the sale. Ask recipients to take a minor step to facilitate future conversions.
  - ° Ask them to click a link to see a client/customer testimonial.
  - ° Ask them to reply to the email to chat with a sales rep.

- Test . . . and never only send one email . . . A-B test everything.
  - ° Test. Learn. Optimize. Repeat.
  - ° Always have a Champion vs. Challenger email running at a minimum of a 90 percent vs. 10 percent list split (use the Champion as the 90 percent).

Below are two sets of examples:

SET #1

- The first is an example of a #1 or #4 email. Very direct. Clear calls to action. Less copy than the second.
- The second is an example of a #2 or #3 email looking to walk the B2C or B2B contact through a path to both establish the value of the program as well as softly overcome objections. **(Emails have been used with client approval.)**

SET #2

- These are email template styles which can be used to highlight a customer success story.
- Appropriate for the Nurturing emails, though they do have a direct call to action to enroll. (**These emails have been used with client approval.**)

The best practices for email design are as follows:

- Design for Mobile:
- Over half of all Email Opens are on smartphone or tablet.
- Clear links and CTAs:
- Make it easy for customers to do what you want them to do.
- Minimize use of images:
- Images should be used strategically and sparingly.
- Compelling copy and content:
- Use short text blocks that link back to additional content on website or landing pages.
- Make it easy to unsubscribe:
- Unsubs aren't great. Undead zombie email addresses are worse.
- Don't slow play your hand:
- CTA or links should be above the fold on desktop and close to the fold for mobile.
- Copy, Content and Design should help to tell the story, not be the story:
- Be compelling, not distracting.
- Have a design philosophy that works with your goals: Grab attention. Add value. Call to action.

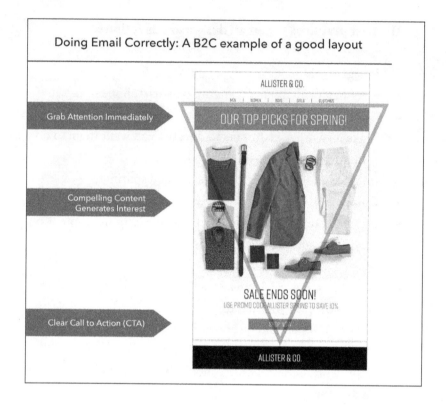

Doing Email Correctly: A B2C example of a good layout

The Standard KPIs for Email Campaigns are as Follows:

- **All Emails**
  - Delivery Rate (Emails Delivered / Emails Sent)
  - Unsub rate (Unsubs / Deliveries)
  - Bounce rate (Emails not Delivered / Emails Sent)
    - ESP should be helping to manage Deliverability
    - Hard Bounce = wrong email address
    - Soft Bounce = temporary delivery problem
  - List growth: Solid engagement metrics (open and CTR) make sustainable growth easier

- **Nurturing Focused Emails**
  - Open Rate (Emails Opened / Emails Delivered)
  - Click-through Rate (Unique Clicks / Emails Delivered)

- Click to Open Rate (Unique Clicks / Unique Opens)
- Time on site

- **Enrollment Focused Emails**
  - Click-through Rate (Unique Clicks / Emails Delivered)
  - Revenue and Number of Transactions
  - Revenue per Email (Total Revenue / Emails Delivered)

Three primary takeaways as you company builds out the email campaigns for new modules:

- Email Strategy—Have a plan for the different emails that you send. Understand that New Module Announcements or Enrollment Email #1/#4, and Nurturing and #2/#3 Emails should all have different goals.

- Email Design—Know your goals and keep them in mind during the Design process. For all Emails, seek to:

  ° Grab attention.
  ° Add value.
  ° Call to action.

- Automate Email Flow Where Possible—Automating customer communication can help to increase leads, conversions and revenue by providing more personalized, responsive and timely messaging. It can also promote efficiency by reducing time required for manually scheduling emails.

8—MEANINGFUL REPORTING VS. VANITY METRICS + ADVANCED ANALYTICS

BASIC REPORTING TO ADVANCED ANALYTICS

The easiest thing to forget about in your marketing and sales teams—aside from making sure there is enough printer toner, and infinitely more important—is their ability to track a person from click to sale and to create actionable KPI reports with a high degree of accuracy.

As a hired agency or an internal marketing team, this is the easiest thing to forget to do. Why?

This is the *least* sexy stuff in the marketing world. It *rarely* sells anyone on an agency or gets anyone kudos internally, though it should. It's surprisingly expensive to hire good people in marketing who can and will do this correctly, and there are few of these people available in the first place. And the job of putting tracking pixels in the right place (hint: everywhere) and setting up a systems to pass data (See Chapter 2, Google Tag Manager) is tedious work.

And I can tell you from my experience, there are days that my agency strains under the burden of making sure there is enough talent and focus to be exceptional at the core "backend" tasks, those tasks that make the numbers move from the top of the funnel, through the sales process, into your CRM, and back to some data warehouse or system designed to help you create actionably, accurate KPI marketing and sales reports.

So you can imagine, if it's this easy for professional digital agencies to forget about doing it, it is even easier for an internal marketing and IT team to not do it.

This being said, if you are in fact *not* doing this, which if you go back and read Chapter 2 again is highly likely, you can't grow your marketing and sales efforts in an intelligent, data-driven way. Simply, you will be flying blind and guessing more than strategizing.

So what do you need to start and what do you need to do before you try and get more advanced?

1. Review Chapter 2's sections **Essential KPIs and Essential Marketing Tracking and Reporting Tech Elements.** Those tactics and pieces of reporting technology and assets must be present in your digital advertising and websites/landing pages so that the data you need actually exists.

    Correct data pass means there is advertising spend, impression, and click data being pushed into the lead record, and that lead record follows a prospective person completely through the sales funnel until they become a mature client. This requires deploying tracking assets such as Google Tag Manager across your entire website, landing page, and digital advertising ecosystem.

    Then, you need to make sure that the CRM you are using is actively updating the original lead record with new sales touchpoints, such as first conversation, meeting, first sale, and any subsequent customer actions.

    Finally, this means that you need to marry the front end marketing data (the money spent, the clicks and the impressions) with the CRM data (the lead being created, the sale) to get the metrics we listed above.

    Most importantly, it is highly unlikely, unless you have an advanced IT department or a weapons-grade digital agency, that this has been done correctly.

    Spend the money and do it right.

2. As we've discussed above, first start with simple marketing and sales campaign performance reports and demand the following from your teams:

a. The cost per lead of each campaign, by ad channel and by product or service line. When this is established, get more granular—as long as the sample sets are high enough, meaning if you have enough traffic and leads coming in—to dive into the by ad channel by campaign by either ad group (if it's search engines) or ad sets (if it's Facebook). Other ad platforms have their different terms for what they call the "level below a campaign," but it's the same idea. Go deeper when you can, and do it when there's enough volume of activity in either dollars or leads to warrant looking at campaigns at this level.

b. The cost per sale or cost per acquisition of each of the items above. This should likely be your ultimate KPI of your marketing and sales world.

c. The prior 30-180 day trends of each of the above.

3. Your next move will be to get fancier. That's fine. Just make sure, per the intro to this section, you do the simple reporting things first and do them right.

The next likely step is to consider onboarding a business intelligence tool ("BI tool") which not only automates the baseline reporting above, but also gives you near-real time reports in typically a very nice web-based dashboard and, most importantly, allows you to easily create new reports and actual analytics that can tell more of a story instead of just showing performance.

The most popular BI tools are Tableau, QlikSense, and Microsoft's Power BI. All are fine, though I personally prefer either Qlik or Tableau.

WHY A BI TOOL?

A BI tool or platform will help automate the now-common baseline reports that are essential to running and optimizing your marketing and sales teams. They also provide the computational power and sophistication to allow you to do more advanced analysis into your operations, and will make new views of the data available very quickly.

One of the most essential things that will start becoming a true differentiator for marketing agencies and companies doing advanced digital marketing is the ability to build and intelligently use a zero-sum attribution model.

We've mentioned this buzzword before, but now let's dive deep and walk you through the basics.

Attribution Models = No customer in the B2B or High Value B2C space sees one ad, clicks on it, and then goes straight to your website or landing page, and becomes a new customer. If you don't run an eCommerce business, the one-click-to-sale model just isn't realistic.

And even if you are primarily in an eCommerce environment where customers can put your products into an online shopping cart, they likely have seen or heard of your brand via digital advertising long before the day they bought something.

That's the premise of the oft-incorrectly used—and certainly overused term—*attribution.*

Attribution is the practice where you try and evaluate to many different marketing channels how much influence they had on a particular sale or overall category of customers, and attribute a value to that effort, typically giving a percentage of the sale or revenue or profit to that digital advertisement or digital ad channel.

This theory and attempt to get smarter about which ads contribute to the final sale is massively important. Without considering the path that a customer took to your digital doorstep in the hours, days, weeks, and months before they became a lead or sale or new customer, you're going to always think that the ad channels with the best ROI are the ones that touched the customers last and— most lethally—are *solely responsible* for driving your business. This is dangerously bad data and can destroy your marketing strategy without you even knowing how bad the problem has become, while you seem to be making the right data-driven decisions.

Comments from executives indicate this is a cancer amid your reporting and analytics Most frequent are the following:

- We need to cut display and paid social and spend more in search. They have terrible CPA/ROI.
- Why is the volume of our tradename search leads/sales down Q/Q or Y/Y?
- Why can't our ROI for other channels be as good as SEM?

Ironically, the same people who completely ignore the value of data-driven, trackable, provable, up-funnel digital channels—meaning things you can *see* and *prove* are contributing to sales 100 percent—are the same executives who tend to spend money in offline, traditional media where there is often *zero* ability to track the down-funnel value.

It's like parenting your two kids differently: you get angry that your oldest didn't get straight A's and isn't dating the right person, but you make excuses why your youngest got expelled for stealing a car. That analogy might be a bit excessive, but when we see clients dropping 40 percent of their marketing budget into dumb (e.g.: you can't do accurate cost per sale reporting!) offline marketing, yet get annoyed when the 3 percent of the budget is being spent on display advertising that's quantitatively at least driving leads and attributed down-funnel sales, it's nearly as crazy to my ears.

Without understanding attribution models and committing to the people and tools to choose and build the right one for your marketing reporting efforts, it's impossible to make smart 21st Century digital marketing decisions with your money.

Again, being able to understand which leads and sales can be partially *attributed* to marketing activity *before* someone clicked on something is the key to deploying best-of-breed digital advertising, ROI and growth-focused campaigns.

The last and more advanced conversation in the world of attribution is what *kind* of data model you want to use in your business. Here are some quick notes, without going down the rabbit hole like your marketing professionals and agency experts in the trenches *should* be doing:

- There are different ways to look at stuff that happens to customers before they click on an ad.
- There is value to the right prospective client even *seeing* your ad on Facebook, with a nice pre-roll video and good looking/sounding copy and images/logo. If the person with the right salary, job title, and company printed on their business card sees your ad every morning after logging into social media, there's a value to that and it's more than zero.
- There is even more value if that person sees *and* clicks on that ad, even if they don't buy anything or submit a lead that day: they saw and read your ad, and took a look at information and your brand experience on the landing page.
- Cumulatively, these actions have a value. Just because someone clicked on an ad today does not mean that they go there without some help along the way.
- The challenge is how to logically and mathematically express the impact of these touch points in your unique sales funnel.

The Different Types of Attribution Models

Last Click

Pros:
Easy to use.

Cons:
Ignores anything that happened (and rightfully contributed to the sale) before the last click/thing that happened. Ostensibly thinks that the only important thing was the last thing someone saw.

Why use it?
Easy to report with...someone with zero digital marketing or analytics experience can set this up.

First Click

Pros:
Easy to use.

Cons:
Ignores anything that happened (and rightfully contributed to the sale) before the last click/thing that happened. Ostensibly thinks that the only important thing was the last thing someone saw.

Why use it?
Easy to report with...someone with zero digital marketing or analytics experience can set this up.

Retail

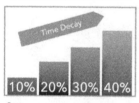

Pros:
Easy to use.

Cons:
Ignores anything that happened (and rightfully contributed to the sale) before the last click/thing that happened. Ostensibly thinks that the only important thing was the last thing someone saw.

Why use it?
Easy to report with...someone with zero digital marketing or analytics experience can set this up.

Positional 40/40 Bathtub

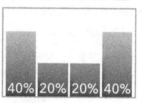

Pros:
Easy to use.

Cons:
Ignores anything that happened (and rightfully contributed to the sale) before the last click/thing that happened. Ostensibly thinks that the only important thing was the last thing someone saw.

Why use it?
Easy to report with...someone with zero digital marketing or analytics experience can set this up.

Linear

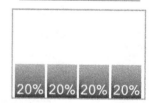

Pros:
Easy to use.

Cons:
Ignores anything that happened (and rightfully contributed to the sale) before the last click/thing that happened. Ostensibly thinks that the only important thing was the last thing someone saw.

Why use it?
Easy to report with...someone with zero digital marketing or analytics experience can set this up.

Again, we must look back at how a real customer's journey looks so we can properly understand the value of looking before the last click and at a zero-sum attribution model:

In a *REAL* Marketing Funnel

In the real world, people see your advertisements across search engines, social networks, banner ads and email campaigns...not to mention offline behavior. And sometimes the ad isn't the right ad or the right time for them to click to learn more...and it's important to understand that seeing an ad has value, but seeing an ad + going to your website/landing page is more valuable

What does this all mean?

It means that your customers are often "born" well before Day 0. In the chart below, this is a fairly accurate view into where a person *starts* to know about your company (it's not the same as the ad channel where they officially get into your outbound sales funnel efforts):

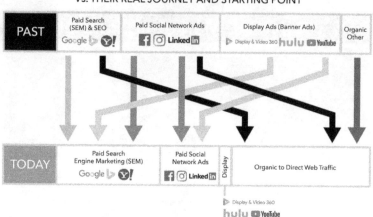

Is your company ready for this more advanced next step in your journey of more actionable and advanced analytics? I would contend that these rather significant investments in your employees' time, your marketing and IT budget, and emotional bandwidth/focus on your company are only worth it if, as we've mentioned quite often, you're 100 percent certain you've got your basic marketing and sales performance reports (not analytics, but core reporting) down cold.

Then, perhaps, if you see the value in what we've talked about above regarding a marketing attribution model, you can take that next, very serious step.

I will conclude by saying that in the next five years, in my opinion this will be the achievement in data within your sales and marketing world that is the game changer and differentiator. To better understand how and where to deploy marketing dollars in the days, weeks and months before your customers know how to find you is going to be the singular greatest ability for (a) agencies to be the best to hire and (b) for your company to be better and smarter than your competition.

I know I'm focused on this for my clients and wish the same best practice obsession with advanced analytics within your company.

CONCLUSION AND CHEAT SHEET

THE GENERAL HIGH-LEVEL STRATEGY looks like this: Humans are advertised at across digital and traditional channels, driven into experiences, and a result is produced and the process is optimized to get more results for a lower Cost Per Result.

In other words, across *all* industries, you need to do the following which incorporates both the Core Four and the Advanced Eight Tactics:

A. Generate new or returning customers' interest via the following ways:

    1. Digital
- a.) Paid Search (SEM)
- b.) Paid Social
- c.) Display Advertising
- d.) Email (often overused, but still plays a *small* role)

The following things can be done via digital channels:
- ▶ Create new leads and qualified sales opportunities.
- ▶ Nurture current leads.

► Nurture current or former customers.

► Retarget visitors to your site to reclaim lost leads and customers.

► Early intent new client prospecting, reaching far "up-funnel" and showing ads online where the message is relevant to your company's product or impressions served to the *right type* of person

2. **Telephony and Offline Marketing and Sales**

   a.) Intelligent Direct Mail using existing database or purchased lists.

   b.) Use automated post-lead generation tactics to support your sales teams like SMS Texts and automated voicemails to ensure, like email, that your customer is being contacted quickly in a professional manner.

   c.) Nurture current leads and customers via the same digital and direct channels listed above. You've already paid good money for leads. It's better to spend money making current leads convert better than to spend money on new leads if you're going to drop the ball with post-lead gen.

The following things can be done via traditional channels (phone, direct mail):

► Create new leads and qualified sales opportunities.

► Nurture current leads.

► Nurture current or former customers.

► Retarget visitors to your site to reclaim lost leads and customers.

► Early intent new client prospecting, reaching far "up-funnel" and showing ads online where the message is relevant to your company's product or impressions served to the right *type* of person.

B. **Make sure those humans convert to a sale or a qualified lead**

1. Use **landing pages** that are surgically tailored to every product line, customer type, geographic location. In the world of 21st Century digital, it's easy to know what exact phrase the human used in Google search to get to your website . . . and you need to have a web experience tailored exactly to that human and talking exactly about the right product or service they are right for.

2. Use **outbound call centers**, whether your main sales team or a high volume contact to transfer (or appointment set), so the minute, hour, or day (depending upon what dialing strategy is proper for your industry and customer) the prospect indicates they might want a phone call, you are doing just that and establishing a relationship.

3. Use **Email** . . . as we discussed in the earlier primer, this is much less a lever for *new* customer generation and more a base best practice to ensure that you are working to build a relationship with each and every lead and prospective customer.

4. **Use SMS Text and/or Automated Voicemail**

C. **Make sure that the sales funnel works—don't forget about what happens after a lead is created!**

1. **Nurture Customers** via one-to-one targeting on social networks. This is not banner ad or social retargeting (that's for net new lead gen). This is helping a lead become a customer. The ad used, the message and the image or the video, must be completely different than a retargeted banner ad because they already indicated interest! And where do they go if they click on an ad? Drive them to a

unique landing page, appropriate for a new lead, which operationally answers the question: What do you want them to do *next*? Then make sure that call to action is heard loud and clear.

2. **Make sure your sales team isn't dropping the ball.** Many times I've heard a CEO say that they "are pretty sure their sales team is partnering well with marketing," and they know definitively that the team has the sense of urgency and the tenacity to take the ball from the 5 yard line => the end zone. It would shock you. Way too often, they are wrong. So I dare you to do some secret shopping of your sales process. Create a fake email account and use your spouse's phone and see what that prospective customer experience is like. You'll be terrified.

3. **Direct mail.** Use this all day long for lead sources or product lines that are high value. Use a direct mail partner and print design that acts like it's been born in this century and not closer to when the Gutenberg press printed its first page.

Again, we cannot forget about the non-digital tactics that are both trackable (i.e.: accountable) and proven to still be effective. Online lead generation via SEM and Social/Display is the core, but you need to both nurture current leads and drive new leads via more traditional approaches, and then test to see what works to support the core digital.

Digital fails sometimes for some products in some markets. It succeeds at a Cost Per Acquisition nearly always better than traditional offline approaches, but it does fail. You just need to have the data to fail quickly, so you can then re-invest that budget where there are good acquisition costs.

D. You know your customer is being driven towards you for days and weeks before they start a conversation, submit a lead, or make a phone call . . . and therefore don't forget to spend money in those channels that drive those eyeballs.

Here's the bottom line for your bottom line CFO-types: If you cut out or under-invest in campaigns like banner ads or social media where you get both a brand lift (millions of times your prospective customers see your logo) and get leads, you are going to kill your pipeline. If you rely on only bottom-funnel tactics, like Paid Search, you're hurting your company because your reporting and view into your sales funnel is too myopic.

The final CEO and CMO level goals should be as follows:

1. **I want you to spend as little as possible with outside agencies,** learn how to do what you can in-house, what should be done by experts, test what will work, then ramp accordingly once you prove a ROI.

2. **Spend what it takes to get critical mass** of new loyal customers in a single market or single product line, if your company is new to the world of digital marketing. Establish a viable and scalable proof of concept, measure, re-tool for your different markets and products, and roll out accordingly.

3. **Build a creative strategy** that is the wellspring for ads, landing pages, shared stories and other brand messaging, to make the Cost Per Acquisition (above) cheaper and is filled with Rich Media First (e.g.: video as standard, static images as backup). Pretty designs often don't sell and convert interest into revenue as well as an intelligent and practical blend of direct messages, simple calls to action,

and crystal clear design and layout. Your customers don't need as much as you think they do.

4. **Fix baseline digital elements** that are low-hanging fruit (ex: Tradename Search) that are currently draining efficiency from paid marketing efforts.

5. **Weaponize creative strategies** to allow paid and organic advertising to scale to millions of potential customers.

6. **Low-Hanging Fruit First.** Why? Cheap, near certain ROI, do it in-house with current "expertise."

7. **At the end of the day, test and learn.** Don't dwell and burn hours listening yourself or marketing experts talk. Do get things and ads and campaigns out the door. Let the market tell you what's working.

Don't forget this list of tactics to employ along the way to supplant a product line or geo or consumer type where and when your demand outstrips what the digital channels are able to provide at a good CPA.

1. **Automated Voicemail** for nurturing efforts. Cheap. Simple. Record a 30-second recap of why your product or service is the best, sent from a unique 800 number that is trackable, and send from one of the many platforms offering this service.

2. **Affiliate marketing**, also called Pay Per Lead ("PPL") vendors. Highly volatile, often non-brand aligned general leads that for some industries are the best and lowest CPA, with the largest volume. Granted, it's only a handful of B2C industries, but this channel is the lifeblood for those under that umbrella—mortgage, insurance, higher education in particular.

3. **Targeted, cheap, but nice looking direct mail** that's not from the 1980s and arrives the day *before*

a retargeting campaign gets launched on Facebook/
LinkedIn and Email.

4.   **Light email.** I hate that email is still thought to be a lever
to pull, a big volume driver for your business, because
it's flat out not. But if done in limited quantities and
timed well with other efforts, it's cheap and a baseline
effort to tie in for nurturing efforts. Doing email and
thus thinking you are "doing" digital advertising is like
singing karaoke and thinking you're up next to open for
the Rolling Stones when they come into town.

5.   **Test a reliable, U.S.-based Q&T call center, especially
for B2C,** and use this as the pre-qualification for any
customer generation effort. Outbound sales teams
are completely different from inbound centers. Don't
hire one to do the other. This can be for both new lead
generation or the #1 most important piece in turning
leads into customers.

Literally every single company in the world should
have a dedicated, trusted, outsourced call center for
outbound marketing. The fact that the telephone is
more antique than humanity's ability to fly, yet most
companies act like their inside sales teams are the right
fit for the job, blows my mind.

Is that saying that an outbound call center for Tiffany's
is the same as the outbound appointment setting call
center for Caterpillar? No. But there's a right size, cheap
outsourced call center for your industry that can make
your marketing and sales funnel ten times more efficient.
don't be like most people, who are too lazy to find it.

6.   **Get your sales team the right messaging.** Make it
consistent. Make it simple. And reinforce it with every
piece of the whole marketing system you're using to
talk to the target B2B demographic.

7. **Finally, demand that the sales team partner with the marketing team (and vice versa)** and learn what they can contribute to the strategy as they talk to the clients, while pushing them to do a better job with reporting, messaging consistency, and communication.

ACKNOWLEDGMENTS

I would like to acknowledge the exceptional people who made this work possible across waves of input, support, and guidance: Prentiss Orr; Patrick van Gorder; Geoff Roebuck; Patrick Patterson; and Tim Fitzgerald; the first person to ever sit me down and teach digital marketing, Marc Prosser; the first to give me a chance in the field, the late Anthony Haney; and the handful of executives and CEOs who showed me you can be a brilliant businessperson and a good human at the same time, including Josh Ogle, Zubin Nagarvala, Sean Fenlon, Casey Cook, and Krish Salam,

To the bosses, executives, and peers who made me better: Kate Kelleher, Dean Penna, John Nuclo, Paul DiDonno, my YPO Forum 11 crew, Bo Anderson, Peter Rush, Suzanne Gamble, Tom Hudak, Michael Arana, Patrick McMullan, and Scott Tavener.

To the hundreds of Level Agency coworkers past and present: Pound for pound, you're the best at what we do.

I want to thank Tom and Cathie Donohoe for the amazing start to life, giving more than they ever should have.

And to Kelly, Ella, and Annie Donohoe for being the reason for every page.

CPSIA information can be obtained
at www.ICGtesting.com
Printed in the USA
BVHW080416080120
568900BV00002B/3/P